REVISITING 52 CHURCHES

EXPLORING THRIVING, STRUGGLING, AND
TRANSFORMING CONGREGATIONS

VISITING CHURCHES
BOOK 5

PETER DEHAAN

Revisiting 52 Churches: Exploring Thriving, Struggling, and Transforming Congregations

Copyright © 2026 by Peter DeHaan.

Book 5 in the Visiting Churches Series.

Library of Congress Control Number: 2026904939

Published by Rock Rooster Books, Grand Rapids, Michigan

ISBNs: 979-8-88809-193-7 (ebook); 979-8-88809-194-4 (paperback); 979-8-88809-195-1 (hardcover); 979-8-88809-196-8 (audiobook)

Credits: Developmental editor: Julie Harbison; Copyeditor: Robyn Mulder; Cover design: Cassidy Wierks; Author photo: Chelsie Jensen Photography

Series by Peter DeHaan

Visiting Churches Series takes an in-person look at church practices and traditions to inform and inspire today's followers of Jesus.

40-Day Bible Study Series takes a fresh and practical look into Scripture, book by book.

Bible Character Sketches Series celebrates people in Scripture, from the well-known to the obscure.

Holiday Celebration Devotional Series rejoices in the holidays with Jesus.

Be the first to hear about Peter's new books and receive updates at PeterDeHaan.com/updates.

CONTENTS

VISITING A CHURCH ONCE IS NOT ENOUGH

RETURN EVERY SUNDAY FOR A MONTH TO GET A BETTER UNDERSTANDING

The goal of *52 Churches* was to visit a different Christian church every Sunday for a year. As people learned about the journey, they became universally excited. Many wished they could go on their own church-visiting sojourn. Some followed my blog posts about the experience, while others anticipated reading the book when it came out.

Friends also plied us with questions:

- What are you learning?
- What was your best experience?
- What's the weirdest thing that happened?
- Are you glad you're doing this?
- Do you miss your home church?
- Are you tiring of your journey? And so on.

Others wondered how my wife (Candy) and I could evaluate a church by attending only one service. You can't. Getting a realistic understanding of a church requires multiple visits.

What if you visit when the service has a business meeting, a guest minister, or a fill-in worship leader? Perhaps the service highlighted a holiday celebration, a special remembrance, or an atypical format. We encountered all of these during our visits. What if the church is between ministers? There will certainly be a different atmosphere under an interim pastor or string of guest speakers. Then it will change again once they select their new leader.

Some churches have a monthly schedule, alternating the style of their services from week to week. This might mean they have a different worship style or schedule each Sunday throughout the month. Other churches have a monthly potluck or special event; that one Sunday will differ from the rest.

Then there are seasonal adjustments. Some have summer schedules and winter schedules, while others have holiday traditions that differ from regular services. To get a full evaluation of a church, multiple visits are required.

I recommend making at least four visits to a church you're considering.

To this point, Church #51 (The Megachurch) asked us to make twelve visits before deciding, but I think twelve is enough to form a habit, so your repetition decides for you.

Our intent, however, wasn't to evaluate churches but to expand our comprehension of worshiping God. Various traditions approach God differently. Each one has something to contribute toward informing a holistic practice of worshiping the triune God.

Despite this, I want to return to some churches. Perhaps we visited on an atypical Sunday, or they had an *off* day that didn't click. Maybe they have other services or meetings worthy of exploring. And, for some churches, I just plain liked them and want to go back.

I'll share these visits as we return to some of the fifty-two churches, along with updates about others. As we do, I'm sure God will reveal more to us, growing us in our faith, in our worship of him, and in our understanding of church community.

Takeaway: Visiting a church once is never enough to understand it. Yet few visitors will give a church a second chance if they make a bad first impression.

Questions:

- When you're looking for a new church, how many times are you willing to visit before you evaluate it?

- What can you do to encourage visitors to your church to return a second time?
- How can you help visitors move into and be accepted by your church community?

[For a brief overview of all fifty-two churches, see the "52 Churches Summary" in the back of this book.]

HOSPITALITY
AND LOGISTICS

We'll begin our investigation by revisiting some churches that can teach us through their embrace of visitors and general management. As we do, we'll also pick up other insightful observations.

A HOLIDAY WEEKEND, LIGHT ATTENDANCE, AND A GREAT TIME
EXPERIENCING SPIRITUAL COMMUNITY

I volunteer twice a month at our local food pantry. Staffed with people from area churches and service organizations, we serve those in need in our community. One Saturday, between clients, I talk with a man who attends Church #2 (Growing Deeper, Not Wider). I ask him how things are going.

They had a packed house when we first visited, holding a business meeting to review their finances, growth, and leader's workload. That Sunday they approved hiring an associate pastor. Since then, they've continued to grow, now having two services, which are both over half full. They soon expect to reach capacity for the second service and near capacity at the first.

In anticipation of continued growth, they recently purchased eleven acres of land located a few miles away.

Part of an old farm, most of the buildings will need to be torn down, though they'll keep the newest barn for storage. They plan to donate the abandoned farmhouse to the fire department for them to use to hone their firefighting skills. I don't know if this practice is widespread, but our all-volunteer fire department will schedule a time to set the building on fire, practice various firefighting techniques, and then control the blaze, leaving only a heap of ashes.

Burning this abandoned building will also limit the church's liability, keeping squatters away and preventing the chance of someone setting up a meth lab there. Unfortunately, that's a very real possibility because the production of methamphetamine is high in our rural area. Abandoned houses provide an ideal place to set up a lab.

The property is on a less-traveled street and, though I know where it is, it's been years since I've gone down that stretch of road. In contrast, I go by their current place a couple times a week. I worry that their future location is not nearly as good as their present strip mall setting. At this time, however, they have no plans to build a facility on their new property. They simply want to be prepared.

I'd already hoped to make a second visit to this church, and this news heightens my enthusiasm.

OUR RETURN VISIT

The opportunity to revisit comes soon.

As an elder, I'm assigned to attend our church's second

service this Sunday, which starts at 11:30 a.m. Though I have no official duties to perform, they want at least one elder present at each service in case something comes up.

This opens our morning, giving ample time to go to the first service of Church #2 at 9 a.m. The drive takes only two minutes, compared with over twenty to make the trek to our home church. Again, there are open parking spaces by the door, unmarked but left open by the regulars so visitors can park close. Expecting to see many people, I'm surprised to see a sparse crowd.

Then I remember it's Memorial Day weekend. We end up with about fifty people, demographically skewing older. (My friend told me the second service attracts a younger crowd.) It's tough when a church has multiple services, as the congregation effectively divides, with only a few people crossing the time-imposed segregation.

One elder spots me and comes up to talk. He recognizes me but doesn't know why. When I mention working together at the food pantry, his confusion yields to recollection. This church sends many volunteers to the pantry and, like this elder, several people will recognize me today but not make the connection of why until I remind them. I don't fault them for this. They're seeing me outside of our normal context, and though I look for them, they're not expecting me.

Their lead pastor is away for the weekend, speaking at another event, leaving their associate pastor to give the message. He wears jeans and a T-shirt, though not one emblazoned with their church's logo, as sported by several of the members.

With no opening worship set, the pastor starts the service. Though I'm only guessing, they may have changed the order of the service so that the worship team doesn't need to be at church so long, with them playing the second half of the first service and the first half of the second.

After some initial remarks, a college student comes up to share about her summer plans: volunteering with Cru. It's not what she had planned to do, but it is the opportunity God provided. She accepts it, albeit with reluctance, as God's path for her. I appreciate her honesty and willingness to be transparent. She needs to raise funds for transportation and incidental expenses. Strategically, she may have been better off keeping her hesitancy from us, but I find her honesty refreshing.

Then the pastor starts his message, discussing poems—and how he wooed his wife with poetry. The book of Psalms contains 150 poems—sometimes raw, overflowing with emotion. "God is okay with us expressing our feelings to him." After making general remarks about the psalms, he reads Psalm 3 but without comment.

The worship team of four comes forward. They sing and play guitar, bass, and drums. Although only two guys use mics for vocals, I appreciate that all four sing. They lead us in three songs: a chorus, an updated hymn, and another chorus. Then they take a break for "connection time."

CONNECTION TIME

Effectively an intermission, connection time is for people to mingle, get a coffee refill or snack, or use the bathroom. Candy and I stand, expectant to talk with people, but everyone scatters. No one comes up to chat, and no one seems available. Then Candy abandons me in favor of a trip to the restroom. There I stand, all lonely and pathetic looking. Fortunately, my elder friend sees my predicament and comes up to talk, rescuing me from isolation. Soon my wife rejoins us. After making the requisite small talk, he pulls a fourth person into our conversation—and then leaves.

With no one knowing what to say, we share an awkward silence. The young lady looks vaguely familiar, but I dismiss this as my imagination. After some more mutual squirming, there's a flicker of recognition. She thinks she knows Candy, having seen her at the local high school as part of the parent association. This young lady, we discover, went to school with our daughter, grades K through 12. With a mutual connection established, we finally have something to talk about.

A personable woman with a broad smile and striking features, she says she normally attends the second service. Today, however, she's a greeter, deciding to go to the first service and then greet people as they arrive for the second one. She points out her mom, who I know from the food pantry, though I'm not sure if she recognizes me.

As the connection time ends, the pastor calls us back. I

assume we'll end the service with more singing, but instead there's part two of the sermon. He shares the story of David and the events that brought about him writing Psalm 3.

After the sermon, he reads Matthew 26:26–27, and we move into communion. I don't know if they serve communion every Sunday, but they celebrated it on both of our visits. Although lacking instruction about visitors taking part, we know from our first visit that communion is open to all. They pass the elements (crackers and juice), and we partake individually, some immediately and some after a time of contemplation.

The service ends, and we talk to more people. As we leave, our new friend stands at the door, greeting people as they arrive for the next service. Her son is at her side, and he's willing to talk to me a bit. Personable like his mom, I ask if he's helping her greet or if she's helping him. He thinks for a moment. "She's helping me!"

With their smiles as our parting memory, we get in our car and head out, not for home, but to go to the second service at our home church.

Today is off to a great start.

Takeaway: An enthusiastic smile can form a lasting memory.

Questions:

- What parting memory do you give to visitors at your church?
- What opportunities does your church provide for attendees to connect with each other?
- Do you play a role in this?
- How can you do better?

STILL SPARSELY ATTENDED
WHERE TWO OR THREE ARE GATHERED

A church that popped up during our initial online search for nearby houses of worship was Church #21 (A New Kind of Church). We'd never heard of them, and no one we talked to knew anything about them. We vacillated about whether we should visit, and when we had trouble finding their location on Sunday morning, I almost skipped them, spotting their small sign on the door only after driving by their building three times.

Although their main room would accommodate a couple dozen, only five people showed up that morning: the two pastors, their son, Candy, and me. They explained that most ministry happens on Saturdays. Having a Sunday service is for the people they meet while doing street ministry. Those unchurched folks expect a Sunday service. Although the sparse attendance presented an initial awkwardness, our Spirit-led time with them was powerful and profound.

On most Saturdays, they start at 3:45 p.m. for a time of "intercession, declarations, and decrees" after holding an orientation for first-time attendees. Next, they offer strategic prayers for our county, state, country, Israel, and the world. Then they take a supper break, returning for praise and worship, wrapping up at 8:30 p.m.

On the first Saturday of the month, however, they start even earlier at 2 p.m.

We first visited them on the Sunday after the month's first Saturday. With over thirty people there the night before, many driving long distances, no one wanted to leave. Their worship lasted well past 8:30 p.m., extending into the early morning. Our pastors were noticeably tired that Sunday.

I wanted to return on Saturday to experience one of their fuller services. Yet with regular plans for most Saturdays, it would be months before I could make a return trip. With my regular commitment to volunteer at the food pantry the first and third Saturdays of every month, it's almost impossible for me to go to their service on the first Saturday, so I picked the second one, showing up several weeks later.

THE SECOND SATURDAY OF THE MONTH

I arrive, expecting to see a parking lot full of cars and people milling about. I see neither. I'm the fourth—and last—person to arrive. That's when I realize that for the full experience, I need to be there on the *first* Saturday of the month. The pastors both recognize me, and one calls me by name, as though she was expecting me. For all I know, she was. As a Spirit-filled follower of Jesus, it's quite possible God had revealed to her I would be there.

Although dismayed at another visit with single-digit attendance, I resolve to make the most of it, expecting another powerful experience. We don't need a lot of people present for God to move powerfully (Matthew 18:20), though it is more fun when experienced with a larger group.

One pastor, aware of my *52 Churches* journey and the book I am writing, gives me some prophetic words. She proclaims my book will encourage others and go deep, serving as a plumb line and a survey—with both vertical and horizontal application. She envisions a chapter on resolutions, which I later add to the book.

"Ask the right questions," she says. She proclaims Candy will write part of a chapter, something the pastor of our home church had also suggested. I later invite my wife to do so, and she does.

Most significant for me was when she says my book "will set people free from denominationalism." This touches the deepest yearning in my soul, for I see denominations as the antithesis of the unity for which Jesus prayed (John 17:20–23). As long as denominations exist, we will never fully realize harmony in our Lord's church. (I even addressed this in my dissertation *The Convergent Church: Moving Toward the Unity for Which Jesus Prayed.*)

She concludes with, "There will be more to do next, after the book." Overcome with hope for the future of Jesus's church, the consequence of her words overwhelms me, as tears of joy well up. For the first time I sense the magnitude of my book and the results of what will follow.

Although they offer the opportunity for active involvement, I take a more passive role, mostly observing and absorbing. What unfolds is not foreign to me but does stretch me. The pastors function at a spiritual level that is only somewhat within my comprehension and barely within my grasp. Maybe next time I'll feel more at ease and will more fully take part.

When it comes time to offer strategic prayer, they offer me first choice: county, state, country, Israel, or the world. All the options loom as too big, too vast for me to cover. I opt for the smallest. They hand me a county map to guide my prayers.

I take the map and sit cross-legged on the floor. I stare at it, looking at familiar names and wondering what to do. The words flow freely from the ministers as I sit mute, listening for the Holy Spirit's direction. Eventually he gives me words to proclaim, haltingly at first and then growing in confidence. The leaders affirm my prayers and add to them. Though my contribution is small, the scope of our collective prayers is profound. The leaders sense God's perspective on a global level, possessing a spiritual perception I seldom see in others. It's a beautiful thing.

With forty-five minutes for strategic prayer, time moves slowly for me at first, but then I ease into the flow of our intercession. Eventually, I am mentally spent, with no more to give. But that comes toward the end of our prayer time, and it soon finishes.

We head to a local restaurant to eat. A few others join the four of us, and we enjoy a great time together, sharing life and embracing God. The food and the break rejuvenate me for part two: praise and worship. I expect it to match my Sunday experience with them—and it does. God's presence fills the room as we sing to him—and for him.

Though the day was powerful, it fell short of what I expected. I'll need to visit on the first Saturday of the month. And I plan to—as soon as I can work it in.

Takeaway: A church gathering doesn't need a lot of people to be meaningful.

Questions:

- Do you have to meet on Sunday mornings to have church?
- What is required to hold a service?
- Does the church staff or the Holy Spirit lead your meetings?
- Who does? Why?

A DELAYED EXPERIENCE
WORTH THE WAIT

We visited Church #36 (The Surprise) as one of our original fifty-two, though I almost didn't count it. On the Sunday we showed up, they canceled their service because their minister had an emergency. With a start time of 11:30, it was too late to head anywhere else. Instead, we hung around and talked with a young friend who was eager to share her faith journey.

Though we had a delightful time celebrating our common faith and God's work in our lives, there was a disconcerting moment when she shared her church's narrow theology. Their resolute view holds that speaking in tongues proves a genuine salvation experience, whereas people who claim to be Christian and don't speak in tongues are deluding themselves and are not true believers.

That statement separated her from us, with her on the inside, part of the spiritual elite, and us missing out. I'm not sure if she would judge us as heathens or heretics for professing a faith that doesn't include speaking in tongues. I'm grieved when a hard theological stance divides the church Jesus started. This isn't what he wanted; it's not what he prayed for when he asked Papa for the complete unity of his followers, that we would be one (John 17:20–22).

Since they didn't hold a church service when we visited, we head back today to experience what we missed. Though I look forward to worshiping with them, I'm also doubly apprehensive. First, my friend's explanation of their church's narrow-minded theology haunts me. Though three of the fifty-two churches shared this perspective, she expressed it the most adamantly. Will they again assault my standing with God? Yet I want to be tolerant. I desire to offer grace and shun possible offense. I pray it will be so.

Second, they canceled service once. Will they do it again? It's a worry I can't shake. Though not purposely planned, we already went to church today, a 9:30 service at our home church. So if this church again cancels their service, I won't feel a void. In theory, we should have had ample time between services, but we don't, with us breathlessly rushing in only a couple minutes early.

BETTER ATTENDED

This time there are more cars in the parking lot, about fifteen. On our first visit, it was bitterly cold and windy, with a hint of snow. Today the sun shines brightly, with the fall temperature above normal. This brightens my expectations.

We open the doors and walk inside, once again to an empty lobby. This serves as an eerie reminder of our first visit. We head to the sanctuary. It's deserted. Instead, people congregate in a side room as they share a meal. Not knowing what to do, we stand for a moment, hesitant. Should we go in or make a quick retreat? As I consider both options and am leaning toward leaving, a man spots us and approaches, struggling to swallow his food so he can talk.

An affable fellow, he shares his name and says he's the pastor. That's odd. Our friend used the title "elder," which I also saw on their sign and in their bulletin.

"Are we early or late?" I'm not sure, concerned we once again missed their service.

The pastor smiles. "If you're here for Sunday school, you're late." His eyes twinkle. "But if you're here for church, you're right on time." His playful demeanor puts me at ease. I immediately know three things: there will be church today, we're not late, and I like this guy.

He offers us food, gesturing to a potluck-arrayed table. I thank him, but decline, partly because we aren't hungry but more so because it's obvious that the time to eat is winding down. He glances at the partially finished bowl of salad in his hands and then back to us.

"Finish eating," I assure him. "We'll just wait; it's okay."

He gladly accepts this and retreats with his salad, but when no one else approaches us, he returns so we're not alone. He redirects his attention to us, smartly balancing his unfinished meal with helpful conversation.

The man looks familiar, though vaguely. His name too seems like one I should know. We eventually discover a common background, having attended the same school. At ten years older than me, he graduated before I arrived; however, his sister was in my grade.

He finishes his salad while others head to the sanctuary. That's when our friend spots us. "I'm so glad you came back." She's sincere, pleased to see us again. Then she apologizes once more for their canceled service on our first visit.

We enjoy an extended time of conversation. Eventually, her husband comes up, imploring her to get ready for the song set. Today he'll handle the A/V, while she leads the singing. She excuses herself to prepare.

By now, most people are sitting, and we join them. It's about fifteen minutes past their scheduled starting time, but no one cares. Aside from us, everyone else was there for the meal and presumably Sunday school before that.

The service opens with singing, led by our friend as she plays guitar. Her sound is pleasing yet carries a distinctiveness I can't discern. Candy detects a slight bluegrass vibe. I disagree but lack a better description. A nearby drum kit and piano sit idle, though some in the congregation use tambourines and many clap. Some people stand as we worship, while others sit.

Though they have hymnals, we don't use them. Instead, we follow the lyrics displayed on the screen up front. Besides hymnals, there are also Bibles in the chairs, the KJV. With seats for over 150, there are about thirty people present: mostly older and predominantly female.

For the opening prayer, everyone prays at once, out loud. It's most disconcerting, with the assault of their words prohibiting mine from forming. All I can do is listen, but I can't make out a single prayer. Their combined cacophony is a jumble of English. If other tongues are uttered, I can't discern them. Later, before the offering, only the leader prays, while everyone else listens.

Three older men (elders, I presume) lead the rest of the service. All three wear suits, the only men so attired, though many of the women wear dresses.

Without being told, everyone stands for the Scripture reading, Hebrews 4:11–16. Then we sit as the minister begins his message. His message rambles, with no theme I can discern, though perhaps the problem is mine. Maybe I'm not focused, as this is my second church service for the morning, and now I'm hungry. He never mentions speaking in tongues, and there's no hint he views it as a requirement for salvation. Throughout his sermon there's much interaction from the congregation, as they react to and agree with what he says, shouting out an "Amen" or "Praise the Lord!" For a small group, they're a vocal one.

To wrap up the service, there's an altar call, and we sing one more song: "Come, Now Is the Time to Worship." It's the only song today that we know. At one point, a woman comes forward and kneels. The three elders surround her. She doesn't look at them or say anything, so they must know her need. The minister lays his hand on her head as the men pray aloud for her while we continue to sing. One by one, they peel away to resume singing. Eventually she returns to her seat. The song ends, and the service concludes. The people mill about, talking with one another.

Many folks welcomed us before the service, and most of the rest share a quick word with us now. Some thank us for visiting, while others invite us back. We talk more with the minister, as well as our young friend. By the time we make our way out, most of the others have already left. We arrive home by 1:00, tired and hungry, but glad to have experienced church with them today.

Takeaway: It only takes one hospitable person to ease an anxious visitor.

Questions:

- Do your church's beliefs alienate visitors and drive a wedge between you and them?
- What can you do to better embrace visitors who hold views of God that differ from yours?
- The essential faith elements should make for a short list. What does yours include?
- Do these core beliefs unite or divide Jesus's church?

OUR THIRD VISIT
MEETING IN A PUBLIC SCHOOL BUILDING

Two weeks ago, we drove around frantically searching for a church to attend, which we'll cover in the Communications and Operations section. Candy suggested a return visit to Church #2 (Growing Deeper, Not Wider). They had just moved from their cozy storefront location in a small strip mall to rented space at the local school, a temporary meeting place as they raised funds to build their own facility.

Unfortunately, we didn't know the starting time, so instead of risking another failed attempt, I opted for Church #4 (Successfully Melding Contemporary and Traditional), which worked out fine, even if it wasn't what Candy wanted.

On our first visit to this church a few years ago, they had one service. By our second visit, they had grown, needing two services to accommodate everyone. Now, with plenty of room at the school, they're back to one service, a 10:30 a.m. meeting. So the timing would have worked out had we headed here two weeks ago, as my bride wanted.

I'm relieved when she doesn't say, "I told you so."

GOING TO CHURCH AT SCHOOL

Decades ago, I went to school here. Out of habit, I pull into the drive I used in high school, forgetting it's now the exit, not the entrance. But with most people already parked, driving the wrong way isn't a problem. Despite there being only one front entrance, a banner hangs over the door to confirm we're at the right place.

The morning is sunny, bordering on hot. I wonder what the gym will feel like. Two greeters, standing just inside, welcome us and hand us a bulletin, complete with a connection card and offering envelope. The meeting space is straight ahead, only a few steps away. There are a couple hundred metal folding chairs on the floor, arranged in three sections. The bleachers can accommodate a hundred more.

"Sit anywhere you want," I tell Candy, forgetting she'll pick a spot toward the front, making it hard for me to observe the congregation. After weaving around a bit, she picks the third row from the front. I groan. With no one sitting in front of us, I feel exposed and on display.

Don, the lead pastor, spots Candy. Smiling, he walks over to talk to us. He often does his work at coffee shops, alternating between several nearby locations. She frequently runs into him at the two closest ones, and occasionally I see him at a third, which is my preferred meeting hangout.

Don follows up with Candy about a recent conversation they've had and then turns his attention to me.

"How's this space working out for you?" I ask.

"Really great! And now that school's out for the summer, we can leave everything set up from week to week."

I appreciate his enthusiasm over rented space, a practice I wish more congregations would consider. I lament churches spending millions to build facilities that are only fully used one or two hours a week. Tapping into existing space is not only practical, but it's also a responsible use of member donations. Despite this, the church has already purchased land for a building and is currently raising funds for construction.

"They turned on the A/C for us this week," Don says. "But I don't feel anything yet."

"I don't either, but it's not too warm. I think we'll be okay." I keep the conversation short, as I don't want to distract Don before the service or monopolize his time.

His parting words are, "Let me know what you think of the service."

I nod, wondering if he really means it.

I spot no one else who appears available for conversation, something consistent with our first two visits. We sit down and wait for the service to begin. In a few minutes, it does.

FAMILIAR FORMAT

The format is the same as our first visit: an opening prelude by the worship band, announcements, message intro, and Scripture reading by Don; then worship. We sing contemporary songs to a soft rock sound. Don has already shared the church's little-known mission statement: "Seeking more worshipers for our God." This reminds me that the focus of our singing should be worship. I've always struggled with that.

After three or four songs, we have connection time, where everyone mingles and chats for a few minutes. Now we have a chance to talk to people. Though this congregation is mostly preoccupied before the service, it's as if they suddenly turn on their friendly switch and will interact with us. Few churches greet well at all three opportunities: before the service, during the service, and after the service. This one does two out of three well, so they're ahead of most congregations—way ahead.

The message comes from Genesis 42, about Joseph, now the second in power in Egypt, seeing his brothers again as they grovel for food. "This is one dysfunctional, jacked-up family," Don says.

Though his expository message is great, I spend most of the time squirming in my hard, too-rigid folding chair; I just can't get comfortable.

Don concludes with the acknowledgment that "Joseph is the right person, at the right place, at the right time."

WEEKLY COMMUNION

The service ends with communion. They've had communion all three times we've visited, so this must be a weekly practice. The first two times, ushers passed the communion elements. Today we go to one of four stations, positioned in each corner of the room, to get our cracker and juice (in small plastic communion cups). We return to our seats to partake privately.

After we sit, I look at my wife and gesture to the cracker and grape juice. "Jesus died for you."

She smiles back. "And Jesus died for you too." We pop the cracker into our mouths and follow it with a splash of grape juice. Then we sing another song, and the song leader prays and dismisses us.

With the service over, we hang around to talk. Though we see people we know, we see few people from our prior visits. The lack of consistency troubles me. While we enjoy the conversations we have, not being able to reconnect with people we met before makes it hard to form relationships.

Since we don't plan to return, this isn't a problem, but had we wished to make this our church home, it would make our transition more challenging. Even so, it's one of the more inviting churches we've visited.

Takeaway: Connecting with visitors is critical if you expect them to return. Even more important is reconnecting with them when they do.

34

Questions:

- What do you think about churches that meet in nontraditional spaces?
- Is having a church building the best use of the money donated to your church?
- If you have a church building, what can you do to use more of the facility beyond one hour on Sunday mornings?
- How can you better use it for community outreach and connection throughout the week?

A SURPRISING END TO
A PROMISING START
A RETURN TO MEETING IN HOMES

Church #7 (The New Church) does indeed move, as planned. They're now a scant 1.3 miles from our home. The move doesn't happen as quickly as they hoped, but it doesn't take that much longer, either.

Their new location is a substantial improvement over their old one. Before, they met in an aging building, a former strip mall in ill repair and lacking any curb appeal. Though they are again in a storefront, this one is newer and more inviting. They moved several months ago but only recently had a *grand opening*.

I want to check things out and see what else has changed. Unfortunately, before I can, they close. I email the pastor to find out what happened. He never responds. An employee at a nearby business says they decided to meet in homes to save money on rent. Interestingly, this group started out meeting in homes.

Although their sign is down and their storefront is for rent, their website lives on, even though they've not updated it in months. It still proclaims they have Sunday morning services at their now closed location.

I'm saddened by these developments and the lack of communication.

Takeaway: Keep your website up to date and be sure to respond to all emails (and voicemails).

Questions:

- How important is it to have a church building?
- Do you think it's as important to God?
- How comfortable would you be meeting for church in someone's home?

STYLE AND SUBSTANCE

We'll shift our attention to revisit some churches that can inform us through their approach to ministry and the essence of their practices and beliefs.

SEEKING THE FULL
PENTECOSTAL EXPERIENCE
EXPECTING THE UNEXPECTED
AND STILL BEING SURPRISED

When we visited Church #14 (The Pentecostal Perspective), I expected more. I expected to experience the movement of the Holy Spirit, prophetic words, and the possibility of people being slain in the spirit. I braced to hear holy laughter and the tumult of the masses simultaneously praising and praying to God in their spiritual languages.

In short, I prepared to be uncomfortable. Yet none of these things happened.

Aside from a couple of phrases publicly uttered in a language I didn't understand and the possibility of some subtle praying in tongues, the service was remarkably non-charismatic. Yes, the worship music was energetic, perhaps with more gusto than some might appreciate. Though I felt a stirring, I couldn't discern if it came from the emotion of the music or the movement of God's Spirit.

While there, we enjoyed close community, taking part in multiple God-centered conversations. Our time with them was a spiritual experience, we worshiped God in the Spirit and in truth (John 4:23–24), and our understanding of the Almighty grew. But I felt I missed the full Pentecostal experience.

The first clue came while talking with a friend. At half my age, she exudes enthusiasm and a zest for God. Her ever-present smile shows how much she loves life; it's infectious. I may have mentioned I expected a bit more from the service, but even if I didn't, she addressed my confusion. "You need to come back tonight," she gushed. "That's when us Pentecostals get really wild."

I wanted to, but we had a conflict, as we do most Sunday evenings. I explained this, promising to return the next time our schedule permitted. She accepted my excuse, but likely assumed it was just a socially polite response, carrying no intention of following through.

Two months later, the opportunity to return on a Sunday night came, but we went to a movie my wife wanted to see. A few weeks later, our schedule opened again, and we saw another movie, this time one I wanted to see.

In discussing this, it became clear I was more interested in the full Pentecostal experience than my wife—much more interested. One Sunday evening, Candy and our daughter

went to a concert, while I made a return trip to the
Pentecostal church.

GOING SOLO

It's hard enough going to an unknown church with a friend.
It's even harder to go alone. I remind myself, however, that
I've been there once before and know a few people. Still, I'm
tentative—actually, I'm trembling. My gut rumbles, and my
heart thumps. Do I truly want to experience them getting
really wild?

It's dusk when I pull into the parking lot. This only
heightens my disquiet. I persist. Walking in with a lady who
parked near me, I attempt conversation along the way. This
calms my nerves. Once inside, I'm welcomed by the same
person who greeted us on our first visit. He lavished attention on us then, making us feel comfortable.

He and I immediately recognize each other but cannot
recall names. It's nice to see a familiar face. He's pleased to
see me again. I share my name, and he reciprocates.

"I've come back to experience one of your evening
services."

He nods, suggesting he understands the implications.

I walk into the sanctuary and sit in the back row.
Memories of my first visit flood back. I appreciate the large,
rectangular space: open, with a simple, yet elegant feel.
During my first visit, I suspected the worship team was an

anomaly in terms of its size, talent, and energy. Tonight, an equally large, accomplished, and energetic group leads us.

There are about forty-five people present. This is much less than the morning service, but most churches experience a sharp decrease in attendance for their evening gatherings —assuming they even have one. The format of the service is the same as before: an extended music set, a time for prayer, a lengthy message, and an invitation at the conclusion.

I enjoy the songs and the singing, feeling the freedom to raise my hands in praise of God. I spot my young friend several rows up. It seems she's having an extraordinary time. With sparkling eyes and a glowing smile, joy emanates from her face. Though several are dancing, her movements are more demonstrative, while remaining respectful and appropriate. I wish I could offer a beautiful performance of physical worship for God, but I can't. My body refuses to find the rhythm to even sway, but my heart dances on the inside.

We sing for about forty-five minutes and then the bass player transitions to the center of the stage. That's when I recognize him as the worship pastor. One of his team led us in song—and she did so with much skill. Tonight, he will give the message, as the head minister is out of town, addressing a different group.

The worship pastor is a confident speaker, dynamic and commanding, much like his boss. Another trait they share is speaking loudly, bordering on screaming. He doesn't need a microphone but uses one anyway. I'm not sure why some preachers feel they need to yell their message. For the fortunate sake of my ears, his fervor eventually decreases to a tolerable level.

Throughout his hour-long sermon, he shares many convicting thoughts, but his message lacks structure. I'm unable to discover a central theme, aside from "worship." To my amusement, he begins with the same verse and teaching I heard at a different church in the morning, 1 Peter 2:9: "But you are a chosen people, a royal priesthood, a holy nation, God's special possession, that you may declare the praises of him who called you out of darkness into his wonderful light." *Is God trying to tell me something?*

Partway through, he makes the thought-provoking statement: "Worship is for us to edify God, and the sermon is to edify us." I need to contemplate this—and I still am.

ADDRESSING VISITORS

Several times he singles out *visitors*. This is not in a welcoming manner but feels more confrontational. I wonder if there are any other guests. Am I being targeted? Perhaps I'm inferring too much. Or maybe he has the perspective that visitors are by default sinful outsiders in need of a Savior.

As he winds down his message, it morphs into a rant. "We need to worship *despite* how we feel." He implores the church to do better. He chastises them for not worshiping

God as they should. They're holding back and not engaged. He says there has been little in the way of healing, prophecy, or Holy Spirit activity in the past few months. He blames this on their substandard worship.

From my perspective the worship was wonderful, some of the best I've experienced in a long time. He feels differently.

Then he reveals that his son needs healing. They've said many prayers, but the hoped-for restoration hasn't happened. If only the worship were better, healing would occur. *Did he actually say that, or did I just think he did?*

Eventually, he concludes. He launches into what I think will be an altar call, and at the subtlest of invitations, all the people surge forward *en masse*. I'm left in the back row. To my left sit his wife and young kids; across the aisle to my right is another couple. I surmise they're visitors. Aside from us, everyone else has gone forward.

The same thing happened on our first visit. Perhaps it's a reverse altar call, where the *saved* go forward, leaving the *heathen* in the pews. The minister addresses us *visitors* in the back. We cannot hide. There's a gulf of empty chairs separating us from the throng of people up front. I squirm, no longer hearing what he says and just longing for his censure to end.

Eventually, there's a concluding worship set, and I gladly resume singing and praising God. My joy returns, but I'm still on guard. Someone approaches the couple to my right, the other *visitors*. Though I can't hear their words, the body language of the talker suggests confrontation. I wonder if I'll be next. Will I be told—consistent with their published theology—that since I don't speak in tongues, I'm not saved and am a lost soul? It's a disconcerting moment.

The service ends. My friend bounds up to talk. We enjoy a great time sharing, and I pray for her. I also talk with others as I make my way out.

The first part of the service, with worship and prayer, offered significant spiritual connection, as did the community afterward. In my journal, I recorded several intriguing thoughts and Scripture references from the message. Overall, I experienced a worthwhile supernatural encounter and am glad for it.

As I leave, I find out this wasn't a typical evening service for them. Apparently, I still haven't had the full Pentecostal experience.

Takeaway: Jesus drew people to him because of his love. Churches should do the same. This applies both to paid staff and to the laity.

Questions:

- Does your church service celebrate visitors or alienate them with harsh words and disconcerting practices?

- Do you try to greet visitors or expect someone else to do it?
- Even if you're not serving in an official role as greeter or usher, what can you do to help visitors feel welcomed and embraced?

LITURGY, GREETING WITH A HOLY KISS, AND THE HOLY SPIRIT

EXPERIENCING A HOLY AWE OF GOD

I awake both excited and unsettled.

I'm excited at the prospect of returning to Church #28 (Intriguing and Liturgical). There's much for me to learn from their mystical worship of God, from their rituals steeped in meaning that I don't yet comprehend.

However, I'm also unsettled, having awakened with a disconcerting feeling of anger. Four times I ask God to remove it from me. Then I change my request: remove this anger and replace it with peace, with a godly contentment. Slowly my angst subsides, and clarity emerges. I had gone to bed with unresolved frustration toward my wife. As I slept, the enemy multiplied it, turning frustration into a roiling anger. All he needed was the emotional door I left ajar. He seized it as an invitation and fomented a full-scale wrath.

Yet God is good. Although it takes some time, he removes my infuriation, replacing it with tranquility.

ARRIVING RIGHT ON TIME

Today we plan not to arrive early at church. With no opportunity for pre-church interaction, we time our arrival to avoid sitting in silence before the service starts. I cut things too close, however, and we breeze in only seconds early. The minister's wife recognizes us and thanks us for returning. Hoping she will again guide us through the liturgy, we slide into the row in front of her. A few more people trail in behind us, and the service begins as the last person scrambles to sit.

Last time, only five people attended. Aside from the minister, I was the only male. Today, not including us, I count twelve people, three of them men.

Panic hits me. Last time we greeted each other with a holy kiss, the most awkward moment out of all our visits to fifty-two churches. Today, not only will I need to give a holy kiss to many women I don't know, but also to three men.

Even more disconcerting, however, is a teenage girl, perhaps the only person there younger than Candy. It seems completely inappropriate for adult males to greet an unrelated teenage girl with a holy kiss. There exists such a fine line between acceptable actions and creepy behavior. I'm not sure whether I'm more uncomfortable for myself or for her. I hope fervently that the minister will skip the holy kiss greeting part today.

My other concern is their incense. I'm extremely sensitive to smells. Last time, just when I feared I'd break into an uncontrollable hack, God intervened, protecting me from being overwhelmed by the repulsive odor. Though the unpleasant smell lingered in my nostrils the entire service, at least it didn't overcome me.

Today, I smell nothing and whisper to Candy, "Do you smell any incense?"

"Oh, yeah!" She gives me a quizzical glance. "Don't you?"

I shake my head. "I guess I'm still congested enough from my cold that I can't smell a thing."

THE RITUAL ROUTINE

With his back to us, the minister moves through his rituals of preparation. As he does, we bounce around the liturgy, aptly guided by the expert whispers of the pastor's wife, who breathes each page number to us just moments before we need them. For his part, the minister moves through the liturgy with deliberate speed, a kind of reverent rush.

The words are familiar to him, but not to me. I'd like him to slow down so I may contemplate their meaning, yet he breezes through them before I can grasp their full significance. Some of his phrases emerge as a melodic chant. I've heard recordings of priests doing this, as well as seen monks do this in movies and TV shows. To me, the result is both eerie and intriguing. In the middle of this, a member reads portions of Acts 16, but the minister conducts the rest of the service.

This portion passes much quicker than I remember. Soon he turns around to share the message, starting by reading from John 17. Again, the contrast between the reverent solemnness of their rituals and the informal, casual delivery of his message jars me.

FOLLOWERS OF CHRIST

"I'd rather we call ourselves 'followers of Christ' instead of Christians," he says. So many people call themselves Christians that it means little—and carries much baggage. Being a follower of Christ shows commitment. It sets us apart.

I agree. Personally, I prefer to call myself a follower of Jesus.

The other thing I jot down is that we need to "pray to the Father, seek intercession from the Son, and appeal to the Holy Spirit." I'm not sure if he's advancing a theological distinction or merely encouraging us to comprehend God as Trinitarian, that is, as three persons in one. Indeed, my prayers became enlightened when I began praying to specific members of the godhead, according to my understanding of their character. We must balance this, however, with the acknowledgment that as a three-in-one entity, praying to any one of the facets effectively communicates with the other two.

HOLY COMMUNION

The message is brief, and soon he's reeling off announcements. Then he begins the mystical overtures for Holy Communion. When he's ready, the small congregation lines up, side by side, along the front. I can't remember if we partook the last time. I consider just observing, when the minister's wife whispers that if we're baptized in Jesus, we may take part. To remain seated would imply we're not baptized, so I go forward to confirm we are. We join the end of the line.

The people cup their hands to receive the bread and eat it immediately. We do the same. Then he moves back to the beginning of the line with the cup.

We squirm at the thought of a shared Communion cup. I consider our options: We could sit down and skip the wine. There's a precedent of sorts. Church #35 (A Well-Kept Secret) only did half of communion, offering the bread but no wine. Or I could cross my arms over my chest to receive a blessing, as instructed at Church #32 (Commitment Sunday and Celebration), but what if this confuses the minister? Of course, I could conform to their practice and slurp from the cup like everyone else. Instead, when he gets to me, I give my head a slight shake and hold up my hand as unobtrusively as possible.

He understands. "Oh, you just want a blessing." Before I can agree, he makes the sign of the cross on my forehead and does the same for Candy. Relieved to have bypassed drinking from the shared cup and avoided calling undo attention to ourselves, we gratefully head back to our seats. That's when he stops us.

"Next time, you can just dip the bread in the wine. We call that intinction." I nod to show I understand. With all eyes upon us, we slink back to our seats.

I think we may have avoided the holy kiss part, but he squeezes it in. Though I don't end up kissing all twelve people present, I kiss too many—way too many.

I discover people do this with varying degrees of compliance. The minimal interaction seems to be merely touching cheek to cheek, without lip action or smacking sounds.

The teenage girl avoids me, and I'm grateful. One woman, whom I know from the food pantry, doesn't know what to do seeing me in an unfamiliar venue, so she merely mouths "Hi" from a distance. Reluctantly, I share a holy kiss with one guy when he approaches me, but not the other one or the minister. With the awkwardness of the holy kiss behind us, we sit down to conclude the service.

There is more liturgy and more ritual. The minister wraps up his part and exits. Then his wife extinguishes the rest of the candles, and she leaves too. Slowly, others depart the sanctuary in silence. Some people place offerings in the receptacle by the door. Though I never gave an offering at any of the fifty-two churches we visited, God prompted me to do so today. I drop off a check as we leave the sanctuary, the last to do so.

THE AFTER PARTY

We don't leave the building, however, but head to the other side of the small structure. We share a snack and conversation. The minister gives us his full attention. Candy enjoys his storytelling ability and knowledge of church history. I, however, grow weary of his rapid-fire delivery that seldom finishes one thought before moving to the next, leaving no room for me to ask questions or interject.

He declares that in two thousand years, no one has ever gotten sick drinking wine from a gold cup. While it may be true, I still view the practice as unsanitary.

He also talks about the importance of liturgy, as it ensures that all aspects of faith are addressed in their worship. Emanating from the fifth century, everything they do has meaning. *Why use fifth-century practices?* I wonder, but don't ask. *Isn't the Bible a better standard to follow?*

He offers to lend me a book that explains their practices. I'm tempted but decline with the excuse that I'd likely never read it. I also remember the book loaned to me that explains the Catholic theology behind the Holy Eucharist. It proved inaccessible and bored me.

Throughout the pastor's stories, a recurring theme is the work of the Holy Spirit in his life and ministry. At times he seems charismatic and an enigma for this most traditional, liturgical church. This encourages me. It also reminds me of the danger of making assumptions about people and churches based on labels. While labels can help in our basic understanding, they can also mislead. May our common focus remain on Jesus as we make all else secondary.

As his monologue continues, the people trickle out. Eventually only he, me, and our wives remain. Undeterred, he continues to talk as his wife locks up the building and we walk to our cars. Though my better half enjoyed listening to him, I wearied of it.

Two and a half hours after arriving, we head for home, in more awe of God and his diverse church, along with a greater appreciation for liturgy and tradition.

Takeaway: Whether we embrace tradition and liturgy, our church practices should generate a holy awe of God.

Questions:

- Considering your church service, what practices do you accept as normal that might be an issue for visitors? (Hint: Most churches have at least one.)
- What can you do to correct this?
- If leadership continues the practice, how can you minimize visitors' concerns?

THE MODERN CATHEDRAL
A SIMILAR EXPERIENCE BUT DIFFERENT

Our area's megachurch holds two services in their mega-building, one at 9:30 a.m. and the other at 11:30. Also at 9:30 is a concurrent service in the original building on their campus, a modern cathedral built by the original owners.

MULTIPLE SERVICE OPTIONS

When we first visited Church #51 (The Megachurch), we didn't know about the concurrent service, but our tour guide shared the key details. The concurrent service has its own worship team that is "a little less rock and roll," with the message from the main service presented via video. Though unintended, the cathedral attracts an older crowd. None of these characteristics appeal to me, but I want to experience a service there anyway. I also wish to hear a typical message from one of their pastors, since the week we visited they squeezed a seminar teaching into the service.

Another intriguing option is a second campus they had started in a nearby city. Its format was also live worship and a video message. Meeting at a local middle school, the service started at 10:30 a.m. I even consider making the forty-five-minute drive to experience it too. But when I go online to verify service times for the cathedral, there's no mention of the other location. I assume it didn't work out. I'm disappointed they couldn't develop a following there.

This isn't the only thing that disappoints me. At Christmastime, this church contacted the food pantry where I volunteer. They offered to deliver Christmas dinners to any of our clients who wanted one. We were dubious, but they assured us of their commitment. After we signed up many of our clients, the church backed out. I'm not sure where things fell apart, but the result was frustration from our food pantry leaders and disillusionment from our clients. As a result, this church made many negative impressions—both for themselves and for Jesus. I lament their misstep.

Despite this, I'm excited to return today. It's summer, so I expect a lighter crowd but am still surprised there isn't a police officer directing cars at the intersection. But the traffic flows fine without one.

Rain begins on our way there, increasing in intensity as we draw closer and unleashing a torrent just as it's time to go inside. Even with an umbrella, I'm wet by the time we reach the main door. I pull on the handle, but the door doesn't budge. Getting wetter by the second, I don't take the time to see if it's locked or just stuck.

"I saw someone go in the side door," Candy says. "Try that one." We head there, and a man standing on the inside opens the door for us as we approach. He and his partner greet us warmly, sharing their names and asking ours. Their friendly, easygoing demeanor sets me at ease, helping me push aside my frustration at being wet and not able to open the main doors.

SMALL AND INVITING

As we head inside, I'm shocked. Despite the impressive size of the building, there is little seating, perhaps enough for 150 people, a fraction of what their main facility holds. Smartly arrayed inside the formality of this dramatic, modern cathedral, is a casual and inviting arrangement of chairs, couches, tables, and accessories.

No one seems available to talk, so we sit down. Candy soon abandons me, however, when she spots their coffee counter. Eventually I head over to wait with her, but before I reach her, someone comes up to welcome me. Candy soon joins us, and we talk some more before our new friend excuses herself to join the worship team. Another lady stops by just before the service starts. We have a short but nice conversation with her too. I later learn she's married to the site pastor.

The countdown counter reaches zero, and the service begins. It's a typical contemporary worship band, with guitar, bass guitar, keyboard, and drums. Besides the worship leader, there are two backup vocalists. They produce a soft rock sound. I'm not familiar with most of the songs and have trouble singing along. But part of the problem may be that the words don't always appear on the screen when we need them and are occasionally the wrong ones. Adding to this, the acoustics in the cube-shaped space are horrendous.

The site pastor talks a bit. He finishes, and some video announcements play. He checks the time. "It will be about two minutes before the message starts, so meet those around you. When you see the video on the screen, it's about to begin."

At that point, an engaged church greeting happens. The congregation now comes to life, as many people welcome us. They make eye contact, share their names, and ask ours. But then their attention darts to someone else. We see a former neighbor and try to catch up before the message starts.

LIVE VIDEO FEED OF THE MESSAGE

The video appears on the screen, and people scurry back to their seats. On our first visit, the husband of this husband-and-wife team spoke. Today we hear the wife. She is a dynamic speaker and a gifted communicator. A chic dresser,

I appreciate her eclectic style, but her bold ensemble distracts Candy.

They're in the middle of a sermon series on the "Basics." Today is "Basic #5: Get Excited and Tell Someone." Using Matthew 4:19 as a springboard text, she delves into a fishing metaphor. Our life is like a fishing rod, and the Bible is our tackle box, with the church as a fishing net.

"People will tell us what bait to use, based on their needs and life," she says. "Out of the heart of men, the mouth will speak" (perhaps paraphrasing Matthew 12:34). Her style is compelling, and her presentation, engaging. I quickly forget she's on video and not live in our building. She's the only female minister I remember hearing who didn't read her message. This reinforces my earlier conclusion that this is a church I could be part of—if we were looking for one.

After the message, the site pastor returns and offers an altar call of sorts. Another staff person, the pastor's daughter, concludes the service. However, unlike our first experience at this church—although in the main sanctuary—we don't find people afterward to talk to today. They came and then they left—so we do the same.

We step outside, and the rain has stopped. We bask in the warm sunshine as we drive home and consider the message.

Takeaway: Strive to leave people with something to contemplate as they leave your church service.

Questions:

- What impact do you make on visitors to your church? (This comes from both the leadership and the laity.)
- How often do you discuss the sermon after church?
- Are your post-church comments a critique of the minister and the service or a celebration of God and a call to action?

HOLY SPIRIT INSTRUCTION
WE MUST LISTEN, HEAR, AND OBEY

Several of the churches we visited and revisited mention the important role of the Holy Spirit in our lives. Church #14 (The Pentecostal Perspective) and Church #27 (A Charismatic Experience) talked about listening to the Holy Spirit and obeying him. And Church #21 (A New Kind of Church) modeled it. Listening to and obeying the Holy Spirit is something I aspire to, but it's an ongoing effort with inconsistent results.

It's been some time since we visited Church #13 (A Dedicated Pastor Team). One day the Holy Spirit brings the minister of that church to memory. My Lord tells me he's struggling financially, and I need to send him some money.

I wish I could say I immediately sit down and write him a check. I don't. Instead, I think about it for a while; I wrestle with it for a couple of weeks. It's not so much that my hesitancy to obey causes the delay. Instead, I struggle to compose a note to go along with my check. I desire for him to receive the money well and not wonder about me having some underlying motive. I wish for him to receive it as a no-strings-attached gift, just as we receive God's grace through Jesus's gift of eternal life.

At last, the right wording forms in my mind. I send a check to him, along with my carefully composed note. I drop them in the mail and forget about it.

A few days later, I receive a handwritten thank you note from him in the mail. He says he doesn't have the words to express his gratitude, but he's going to try. He says that he and his family have been struggling financially. He and his wife decided to share their concern with their children in expectation that this situation would help them grow in their faith and see God's hand at work.

As a family, they prayed for God's supernatural provision for their financial needs. Then, my check showed up. It was an answer to their prayers. They celebrate God for supplying what they needed, as they should.

I share this, not to call attention to myself, but to encourage everyone to listen to the Holy Spirit and do what he says. I'm not sure if my lag in sending money aligned with God's timing or if it was nothing other than delayed obedience, but it all worked out.

From personal experience, however, I know that the

longer I wait to follow the inner promptings of the Holy Spirit, the less likely I am to fully obey. Sometimes I comply in part, but not in full. Other times I talk myself out of it, concluding I didn't hear him correctly, or that I misunderstood what he was trying to tell me. I am quite sure, however, that these logical analyses disappoint my Heavenly Father.

I should count this experience as a win—grateful for the results of my effort—but I don't, because the Holy Spirit didn't give me one instruction but two. He also told me the pastor needed a friend from outside his church, and I was to offer it.

The idea thrilled me. He's a winsome individual, and I'm drawn to him. I relish the thought of us periodically getting together. Though we have in common our faith in Jesus, we share few other characteristics. Even so, I delight in the idea of spending time with him to encourage him in ministry, with his family, and in living out his faith.

Yet I don't act on this. Again, I struggle with the messaging. How can I offer him friendship without it sounding as though it's in expectation for the money I sent? That would be exactly the message I don't want to communicate. Failing to resolve this, I don't move forward. I lament that I never figured out a way to make this happen. I also lament that I failed to fully obey the supernatural leading of the Holy Spirit.

In all the churches my wife and I visited for my books *52 Churches*, *More than 52 Churches*, *Visiting Online Church*, and *Shopping for Church*, we never once gave an offering. We had decided from the beginning that we would not do so. We saw only downsides for us and the churches. Instead, we continued to support other ministries without interruption.

I did, however, leave an offering when we returned a second time to Church #28 (Intriguing and Liturgical). The Holy Spirit had prompted me to give, and I was happy to do so.

Yet there was one other time I sent money to a pastor.

When researching my book *Visiting Online Church* during the coronavirus pandemic, I connected with a young minister after attending his church online. I was drawn to him as a teacher and as an effective leader. The authentic way the church offered an online experience to their congregation was among the best that I witnessed. It was simple and genuine, pointing me to God and helping me to better worship him.

I later learn that he and his wife had amassed a lot of college debt in preparing for ministry. The Holy Spirit prompts me to pay their student loans for a month. I do. This time I obey right away and am so glad I did.

The financial needs in our world loom large. It's enough to overwhelm us. Being overwhelmed often leads to inaction. My response when being confronted with the pressing need of an organization or individual usually had one of two extremes. Either I'd respond immediately and later regret it, or I'd ignore them and later feel guilty.

To address this ongoing dilemma, the Holy Spirit leads me to develop a giving strategy. I select four areas—as aligned with my passions and priorities—that I'm to be open to give to. It will be my choice. Everything else I will respectfully decline—and do so without guilt. This includes those who contact me online seeking a handout.

This plan gives me a way to be generous to a cause I align with and decline all others with a clear conscience. The only exception is when the Holy Spirit tells me otherwise. It works amazingly well.

Thank you, Holy Spirit.

Takeaway: In determining which causes to support financially, listen to the Holy Spirit. Then obey what he tells you to do.

Questions:

- Would you classify yourself as stingy or generous?
- What plan do you follow in determining which ministries or causes to support financially?
- What's your experience in listening to the Holy Spirit?

- How well do you do at obeying what he tells you to do?

COMMUNICATION AND OPERATIONS

The third group of revisited congregations explores how churches navigate changes to their schedule and the impact it has on visitors. Along the way, we'll pick up other valuable observations as well.

BAD TIMING, BUT A GREAT DAY ANYWAY

A SECOND ATYPICAL SERVICE

We first visited this small Presbyterian church (Church #43, A Welcoming Church with Much to Offer) several months ago. Then it was a cold winter day. Today, spring permeates the air. But I don't need warm sunshine, blue skies, or the life-promise of burgeoning buds to bolster my expectations. I'm excited to return, eager for the experience.

The day before our first visit they held an ordination ceremony for their new minister, a 20-something recent seminary grad who would fill their empty pastorate. Unfortunately, prior commitments kept her away that Sunday, delaying her official start a couple of weeks. Palpable excitement permeated the congregation. Even the building seemed to exude anticipation, reminding me of

Jesus' words during his entry into Jerusalem on what would become Palm Sunday: "If they keep quiet, the stones will cry out" (Luke 19:40). Okay, maybe that's overreaching—or maybe not.

ANTICIPATION

Nevertheless, I long to return to meet one so anticipated. Today is the day. But it isn't just their new minister that makes me want to return. The congregation's friendliness also beckons.

As we learned from *52 Churches,* the formality of liturgical churches usually overflows to their outreach, specifically their lack of connecting with visitors. Stoic members at some liturgical churches failed to greet us at all, while most other congregations struggled mightily, awkwardly offering only a token welcome. We'd leave their services lonely. Community didn't exist or was at least restricted to established insiders.

Aside from this church, the only other liturgical congregation able to break from this pattern was Church #32 (Commitment Sunday and Celebration). While I salute both that congregation and this one, today's church added exuberance to their embrace. I desire to experience it afresh, all the while hoping our first visit wasn't an anomaly.

In addition, this church also earned my appreciation for making their liturgy accessible to outsiders. While we stumbled through the services at every other liturgical church, this one had everything we needed in their bulletin, allowing us to follow along and engage in their service.

Another trait that stood out was their attitude. Despite being mostly older, they have a youthful demeanor. I'm not against aged congregations or people, but I enjoy being around those who, regardless of their age, are full of wonder and expectation. This group exemplifies that. All these memories bubble up in my mind as we drive to church.

I can hardly wait to get there. As we walk toward the door, the wind threatens to blow us away, as if opposing our entrance. We lean into it to make progress. The normal angst I always feel when visiting a church rumbles in my gut.

Just get to the door, I tell myself. *Once you're inside, you'll be okay.* I take a deep breath as I open the door for Candy. Catching my reflection in the glass, I try to corral my wind-blown hair as I follow her inside.

MEMBER LED

Two couples, poised to greet us, flank the narrow entrance. They all look familiar and try to welcome us at once. Though disconcerting, I much prefer it to being ignored. Their embrace warms me, and even more so the man to my left.

"You were here before. I'm so glad you came back!"

"And it's good to be back!

"You were the one visiting different churches and blogging about it, right?"

"Yes, I am! I'm honored you remembered." Though I always told people about our journey of visiting churches, I seldom said I was writing a book and don't remember ever mentioning my blog. The man must have found it on his own.

"We were here just before Sara started. Everyone was so excited. I wanted to come back and meet her!"

"Oh, no!" he says. "Sara's gone this week."

"That's terrible!" I should have tried to mask my disappointment, but I didn't. My mind whirls, and I miss what he says next. "Well, it's good to be here, anyway." I pause, waiting for them to offer us nametags, knowing it's their practice. When no one does, we move forward. Only then does someone remember.

"Oh, nametags. We've got to get you nametags . . . Do you want nametags?"

I nod as I scan the foursome. None of them have theirs.

"Oops," says the first man. "We forgot ours."

Candy prints our names on adhesive welcome stickers, while the others retrieve their premade tags from the board to my left. By the time I affix mine, we're all wearing nametags.

Configured the same as last time, the sanctuary feels smaller than I remember. We make our way in, and more people greet us. A few remember us. They either have few visitors or wonderful memories. Regardless, their recognition embraces me. It's as if we've returned home.

I count twenty-five people, about half the number as last time. I ponder the implications. Invariably, some people leave when a new minister arrives, but usually many more return and new people show up. I expected to see more, not less. Yet if anything's amiss, there's no hint of it.

One member greets the congregation to begin the service. He details all those who are gone this week, while acknowledging visitors. He looks in my direction, and I nod. I wonder if the explanation for low attendance is for our benefit.

I clutch my bulletin, knowing it's my lifeline for participating in the service. This time, I'm mindful to keep the pages in order. Though the rhythm of liturgical services still eludes me, I'm closer to being engaged today than ever before. Perhaps given practice, I can learn to embrace liturgy.

I really appreciate that the members conduct the service. Besides today's liturgist, other members also take part. Though we see today's guest speaker, he merely sits through the first half of the service, while the members lead. This is how it should be. The only thing lacking is for one member to give the teaching as well.

GUEST MINISTER

The guest minister is an associate at the area's largest Presbyterian church and a familiar face to the members here. He stands to give his message, "The Gift of Recognition." We read Luke 24:13–35 about Jesus and two disciples on the road to Emmaus after his resurrection. At first, the disciples don't recognize him.

The minister is a gifted teacher, pulling out insights I'd never considered. It's been a long time since a minister has dug deeper into the text than me. At best, I leave a service with one new thought, but not this Sunday. Today I note several new items he pulled from this narrative:

- They have all the facts, but they are clueless about what they mean.
- They tell Jesus about Jesus.
- With life there is hope; with death there is no hope.
- Even when Jesus taught them, they didn't understand.
- Only death is fed by despair.
- Certainty is the enemy of faith.

He ends by saying, "Let us cultivate the spiritual discipline of recognition." Though the context is recognizing Jesus, the people of this church did a fine job recognizing

Candy and me. Oh, how sweet it is to be seen. May we do so for others but especially with God.

After the service, they invite us to stay for refreshments. We make our way to the kitchenette, enjoying conversation along the way. The food is incidental.

Nick, who greeted us when we first arrived and was today's liturgist, invites us to come back again to hear Sara.

"Her style is very different from what you heard today." I understand this as a compliment. Then he whispers a date next month when Sara will be away at a denominational meeting. He's responsible for finding a replacement and has been turned down five times. "June is a hard month to fill."

"You don't need a guest minister." I want to encourage him to break that expectation. "You can have a member speak."

He's skeptical but then recalls a service they held without a pastor, where the members took turns sharing. "There wasn't a sermon."

"You can do that again!"

He's not so quick to embrace my suggestion, but pauses, as if contemplating it.

The crowd dwindles. We say a collective "Goodbye" and head out, happy for this time of celebrating Jesus with them.

Takeaway: Make sure that your service and your members embrace visitors.

Questions:

- When a church service doesn't go as you expect, how do you react?
- Do you think your response to the unexpected honors Jesus or disappoints him?
- How well does your church embrace visitors when your minister is gone?
- Can your church hold a service without a minister?

A NEW BEGINNING

THE THIRD TIME IS THE CHARM

Three weeks later is Memorial Day weekend. Holidays are a bad time to visit a church. Seldom is it a representative experience. The wise decision would be to attend our own church, but I know to expect our B-team on holiday weekends. That's not a complaint, as much as an observation—and a common occurrence at many churches.

We've already visited Church #43 (A Welcoming Church with Much to Offer) twice and know what to expect. With our goal of meeting Sara, their new minister, returning this weekend makes sense. My only concern is that showing up twice in one month will lead some to assume we plan to join their community. We must not raise false expectations.

The weather today is perfect, with the warm sun as a

suitable partner for my mood. We arrive earlier than planned, perhaps a result of my anticipation. A different greeter awaits us. He recognizes us but isn't sure how many times we've been there. After chatting a bit, we stroll into the sanctuary but without him offering us nametags.

Many people come up to thank us for coming back. Not only do I recognize faces, but I also remember some names. Aside from their friendly outreach, everything else about this church is the opposite of what I prefer, yet something draws me to them. Even though this is only my third visit, I'm already comfortable here. It feels like home, and these people, like family.

One person scurries over, horrified no one offered us nametags. She's eager to correct the oversight, and we let her. This amuses me. Although nametags are important to them, they stumbled on this for all three of our visits.

THE NEW MINISTER

Now, with our nametags in place and having talked to just about everyone present, we sit. I spot Sara across the room. She's exactly what I expect from her picture, yet she's not at all what I anticipate. Enigma best describes my reaction.

The formal robe she wears seems out of place for one so young, yet she bears it well, carrying herself with poise. Confident, she moves about, conferring with others or offering last-minute instructions about the service—all to people more than twice her age. Amid her solemn countenance, she retains a youthful charm. She exudes peace. I immediately like her.

The service progresses like the other two. When Sara dismisses the children for their activities, they pause at the door. She blesses them, and they repeat a blessing back to us. They leave, and she begins her message, "Contemporary Images for Christian Ministry: Servant Leaders in a Servant Church."

She reads her message and is the best at it I've ever experienced. Her delivery is smooth, with a deliberate slowness. Articulate, she enunciates each syllable of every word with unhurried care. The words she chooses are mature and formal, with a dash of youth underlying them. Only in the few instances when she deviates from her script does her true essence emerge.

Based on Matthew 20:20–28, she teaches about service and serving. She frequently quotes others and weaves in a couple of personal stories. While interesting, I have trouble connecting her message with the sermon title and Scripture reading. However, I can't fault her. Occasionally, I've had an article idea that doesn't materialize as envisioned. Yet, with a deadline looming, my only choice is to make it the best I can and hope readers connect with it. Maybe this is her dilemma. Or perhaps the missed connection is on me. "All we need to serve," she says in conclusion, "is love generated by God."

QUESTIONS TO CONTEMPLATE

Before we leave, she offers two items for contemplation. The first is to reflect on God as a server. What should we do to follow his example?

The second is to think about where we are serving now. If we're not serving, where should we serve? If we are serving, is it the right place? Do we need to make changes? Do we need to serve more? How is God directing us?

These are all good questions. I'm not serving as much as I once did. Am I in the right place, doing the right things for the right reasons? Is God pleased with my service or disappointed? I'm glad for the nudge to consider this. Her strong ending more than makes up for what I may have missed in the middle. She hit a home run with me.

As we mingle afterward, it's clear many people hope we'll become part of their community. Someone invites Candy to join the choir. Another tells us about a bus to take us to their upcoming biannual denominational meeting. They invite us back next week for a special outdoor service. They tell us how they want to grow, and how they yearn to attract younger people. I wonder if they consider us young.

Eventually we talk with Sara, sharing about *52 Churches* and our past visits to this church. Hers is a winsome personality, simultaneously mature yet youthful. She's a great fit for this congregation, and I see why they looked forward so much to her arrival. We have an engaging conversation, and I'd like it to continue but feel we're monopolizing her. Yet each time I try to wrap up our interaction, we find one more thing to talk about.

By the time we make it to our car, it's 11:45. Assuming an hour-long service, we talked for another forty-five minutes, but it didn't seem nearly that long. It seldom does when enjoying genuine community with other followers of Jesus.

I'm so glad we came back a third time.

Takeaway: Attitude is everything. Make sure you have a good one.

Questions:

- Is your attitude contagious?
- Where can you serve at church?
- Are you serving in the right place?
- Do you need to serve more, or are you overcommitted?

ANOTHER CANCELED SERVICE
A FAILURE TO COMMUNICATE

I enjoyed the worship at Church #27 (A Charismatic Experience) and appreciated their charismatic demeanor. Yet I was also critical of most other aspects of their service.

Candy said I had a negative attitude, with my perceptions tainted by a former member who had a painful experience there. He left scarred and disillusioned, often sharing his angst with me as he processed his time there and later his distressing departure.

She may be right. She probably is.

Given this, I want to return, praying I'll have an open mind this time. Her addendum to my pre-church prayer is more specific: that I'll forget the things my friend told me about this church and their leader.

Full of anticipation, we arrive early to find an empty

parking lot, despite their Facebook page confirming a 10:30 a.m. service. My heart thumps within my chest. Panic hits me. Doubt assaults my mind. Did I get the time wrong? Did they move? Am I working under a wrong assumption? Perhaps they've closed.

Apparently, they canceled their Sunday morning meetings for the summer, replacing them with evening worship. This is what we infer from a small handwritten note taped to the door. How disconcerting. My initial panic gives way to irritation. And all my friend's disappointments with this church flood back into my mind.

We have plans every Sunday evening for the rest of summer, so it won't be until fall when we can come back for a morning service. Assuming we even try. Do they deserve a third chance? I suppose so, but the real question is, will I give them another try?

This also presents an immediate dilemma: where do we go to church this morning?

Takeaway: Publicize changes to service times (or location) and update all communication channels.

Questions:

- What do you do when you have a critical attitude about a church? Or about *your* church?

- When you change service times, how well is it communicated?
- How does this change impact people who show up at what they think is the right time and you're not there?
- What can you do to be there for those people?

A MISSED OPPORTUNITY
THE SUMMER SCHEDULE

Just down the road from the church that canceled their service is Church #8 (A Grand Experiment). We enjoyed our visit there but later realized it was solely because of one significant interaction we had after the service. The rest of the congregation ignored us, and little else stood out.

When I encouraged a friend to visit the church, not a single person talked to her. She'll never go back. I suspect that's the norm for what most guests encounter, with our experience being an anomaly. At first, I wanted to visit again, but I later decided it didn't matter. Yet today, a return trip seems our best option.

A month ago, we received a flyer in the mail stating they now have three Sunday morning services: 9:00, 10:15, and 11:30. We arrive at 10:17, two minutes late for their second service. The parking lot is full, and one person enters the building just before us. Unlike last time, however, there's no greeter. But there are people milling about, despite most of the congregation sitting in the sanctuary, singing.

A MUSIC-ONLY SERVICE

We can slide into a back row, but before we do, I make eye contact with a woman roaming the lobby. "Did the service just start?"

"No, it's almost over. They'll finish in about fifteen minutes."

"Oh. I thought you had a 10:15 service."

"We did, but we changed times this week for the summer. Now the services are at 9:30 and 11:00."

We nod as we ponder what to do.

"Our minister's gone this week, so we're singing the entire service."

I look at Candy. Her face tells me she doesn't want to stay. "The music's really lame," she whispers. She's right. I don't think I can deal with it for an hour.

I turn back to the woman. "Thank you for letting us know. I think we'll come back when your minister's here." My explanation is merely an excuse to give us a graceful exit, since we don't want to stick around.

A church service shouldn't require a minister or even a message. Church is wherever and whenever people gather, focused on God. But this is a gathering that doesn't do well at embracing outsiders, so we leave. I don't plan on returning, even though I told the lady we would.

OTHER CONSIDERATIONS

Back in our car and having failed twice to go to church, I suggest Church #3 (It Only Hurts When You Care) or Church #5 (Catholics Are Christians Too), both with 11:00 a.m. starting times. Near each other, we drive in that direction as we discuss options.

Church #3 had an atypical service when we visited, so a return trip should give us a more common experience. Yet I don't expect we'd encounter anything new, so I don't really want to go back.

Church #5 was our first Roman Catholic experience. With several friends who attend this church, there's a pull to return. Though hard to follow, with practice we could one day learn to embrace their liturgical services. Given this, another visit would be good. There's too much time, however, between now and 11:00, so we would need to find something to do for half an hour.

As we continue to drive, Candy suggests Church #2 (Growing Deeper, Not Wider), which we've already revisited. Since then, they moved from their storefront location and are meeting at the local school. This also gives them the space to have one service instead of two. Though we think we know which building they meet in (down the street from Church #3), we don't know what time.

My better half wants to try anyway.

I don't. "Let's go some other week, when we can verify the time and arrive early."

She says nothing.

Then we discuss just returning home. Though tempting, we don't.

Takeaway: When people scramble for a church to attend, make it easy for them to pick yours.

Questions:

- If your church has a different summer schedule, how well do you communicate it?
- Does the change in times confuse and frustrate visitors?
- What would your reaction be if your church held a service with just singing?
- If your response is less than positive, what's that say about you? About your worship team?

SEARCHING FOR A PLACE TO GO
ANOTHER CHANGE IN SERVICE TIMES

After striking out at two churches who changed their starting times and dismissing three more, I remember Church #4 (Successfully Melding Contemporary and Traditional), which is next door to Church #5 (Catholics Are Christians Too). I think they have a 10:30 service, and my notes confirm that. We agree to go there, more as a default option than anything else.

With many cars in the lot, the sign out front confirms a 10:30 service. Though two minutes after their starting time, greeters still stand at their post. We exchange pleasantries and receive bulletins. Music flows from the sanctuary, beckoning us in; another family arrives after us and follows.

The service just started. I spot a friend who volunteers with me at the food pantry. He's pleased to see me, with his wife pleasantly surprised at our presence. We scoot into a back row, right in front of the sound booth.

A contemporary praise band leads us in song, mostly choruses. The song leader plays guitar, with his wife on backup vocals. His dad, who's also the minister, plays bass, plus there's a keyboardist, but there's no drummer today.

PHASING OUT ANNOUNCEMENTS

After the song set is announcements. The first announcement is that they're phasing out announcements, since the information appears in the bulletin, in their newsletter, and on the screen before the service. I applaud this. Announcements interfere with the flow of worshiping God.

Ironically, a string of announcements follows anyway. I tune them out, yet one catches my attention. This church and Church #2 (Growing Deeper, Not Wider) will work together to hold vacation Bible school this summer. I'm excited they'll combine resources for the common goal of reaching out to the community.

Next comes a reminder that today is Pentecost Sunday. I'm dismayed that I didn't realize this. A pianist plays as we sing. When prompted, we raise our hands—a strange occurrence for this normally more reserved congregation—inviting the Spirit of God to fall afresh on us, to melt, mold, fill, and use us. In my experience, so few churches make any effort to acknowledge Pentecost. I'm glad this one does and am happy to experience it.

A VOTE TO CHANGE SERVICE TIMES

In another irony, this church is considering changing their starting time. They pass out ballots for the congregation to vote, which they later collect with the offering. After the children's message, the kids leave for their own activities.

Using Solomon's dedication of the temple, found in 1 Kings 8:22-65, as the key text, the message considers the question, "Who is God?" After reminding us that God is omnipotent, omniscient, and omnipresent, the minister pulls other characteristics of God from the text, as well as from other passages.

"It doesn't matter what God looks like," he says. "What matters is who he is." The appropriate response for us is "to be totally abandoned to God."

We conclude by singing hymns with piano accompaniment. Afterward, they offer refreshments. As we mingle, I tell the minister about our ordeal this morning of churches changing service times. That's when we learn the result of the vote: they'll change their time to 10:00.

He's dismayed. Eleven o'clock, he says, is the ideal time for a seeker-sensitive service, but this congregation wants an earlier time to meet their preferences. They'll announce the change next week and switch the week after that.

I hope they'll do a thorough job of communicating the new time and not confuse visitors, as two other churches did with us today—and my home church did too many times in the past.

Takeaway: It's critical to fully communicate changing service times and seasonal schedules. Don't leave visitors driving around and disappointed—or angry. Even better, don't change times.

Questions:

- Does your church do things in the best interest of members or in the best interest of visitors?
- Do you have a member-first or visitor-first perspective?
- Do you have an inward preoccupation with church or an outreach mentality?

CHURCH HEALTH AND LIFE CYCLE

Last, we'll shift our attention to some bigger picture items and peek into the future. As we do, we'll celebrate God at work.

RETURNING HOME
CHURCHES MOVE AND THINGS CHANGE

We started visiting fifty-two churches the Sunday after Easter. We celebrated the resurrection of Jesus at our home church and then slipped away for a year, visiting a different Christian church every Sunday for a year. At least that's the quick way to explain our journey.

We doubled up on two weekends, twice visiting one church on Saturday and another one on Sunday. This way we could visit all fifty-two churches in only fifty weeks. The timing was intentional. By completing our mission two weeks early, we could return to our church in time for Holy Week. Our mission of visiting all these different Christian churches would be bookended with Easter celebrations at our home church.

But that's not quite how it worked out either. I was so eager to return and re-immerse myself in their fellowship that we returned two days early for their Good Friday service. Even so, I count Easter as our official reunion.

I covered our return at the end of *52 Churches*, labeling it as Church #53 (Home for Holy Week). Then I reprised that experience for the opening to the sequel, *More Than 52 Churches*.

CHANGES HAPPEN

Since then, two key things have changed: we've moved, and they've moved.

After being away, we will be back in town on Easter to enjoy Sunday dinner with family—or at least as many of us who can gather at Mom's house. Since we'll be in town for the day, our daughter suggests we visit our former church. Though I have my doubts, preferring to leave it in our past, in the end we end up joining our daughter and her family to check out our old church in their new building. Though I've maintained contact with my closest friends there, I will enjoy seeing others—assuming they still go there.

The church was started a decade before by a group of people who didn't fit into the established church culture. I was one of them. We first met in a traditional-looking church building that seated a couple hundred. After our second week, we had to add a second service.

A few years later, with two services no longer able to contain our numbers, we tried going to a multi-site arrangement but couldn't manage a distributed congregation and staff. We also moved our primary location to another building, bigger and older. Although that building could accommodate twice as many people, in short order we added a second service, fueled by an influx of people as we shut down our failing remote locations, one by one.

Services at the second location were good, but most people acknowledged that something was different. The intense spiritual thrill of our early years, in our first building, was largely gone. Though the music was the same and the key staff hadn't changed, something else had. Theories abounded, such as congregation size, a shift in leadership focus, or the allure of what was once fresh becoming routine. But in the end, we failed to reclaim what we once had. Even so, the new version of our church was still more exciting and more alive than most any other church in the area.

A few years later, with our two services maxed out—and too often over capacity—we looked to move again. This was when my family relocated to another town, and we stopped going to that church.

Now they're in their third building, this one with over twice the capacity of the second. As a converted warehouse, it looks nothing like a traditional church, making the building much more aligned with the church's culture and clientele. Having been in the building less than a year, they've already added a second service to accommodate all the people who want to attend.

HOME FOR EASTER—AGAIN

Today, we head there to check out the new location of our former church. We estimate the drive will take an hour. Being Easter, we expect a crowd, so we add extra time. The day is sunny, the sky is clear, and the temperature is agreeable, especially for this time of year.

Our drive is pleasant as we clock off the miles, making better time than expected and arriving earlier than needed. We're one of the first cars in their main parking lot. Even so, activity bustles around us. Many people are already there, apparently parking in auxiliary lots, leaving the main one for visitors. Inside, palpable excitement permeates the space. My remaining apprehension evaporates as their anticipation of the Easter celebration envelopes me.

Just inside, a familiar voice bellows out my name. Before I can scarcely react, loving arms reach out to embrace me. It's good to be known. My friend and I talk a bit, but there are others he wants to greet, too, so we head on in. Part of me wants to hang out and mingle, but this is no longer my church, and I feel it would be wrong to act as if it were. Instead, we go into the worship area and sit. I take in the space.

The new sanctuary is in the biggest part of the old warehouse, which has the highest ceiling in the facility. The space is rectangular, with it being much wider than deep. Along one wall sits the stage; facing it are four sections of comfortable padded chairs. The room is more spacious than I expected from looking at early designs on paper. The balcony flows nicely and is not as restrictive as I feared. Overall, the room possesses an open, airy feel, comfortable and inviting. Seating several hundred on the main level, the balcony might add another hundred or so. But that's just a guess. Though I want to investigate, I don't.

Background music plays as people migrate in and fill the seats. Everyone is abuzz. I've been gone for nearly a year, and though I recognize many people, more are new to me. By the time the service starts, the main level is mostly full.

The worship team, comprising a familiar cast of talented musicians, kicks off the service, leading us in a series of modern praise songs. The worship leader wrote some of them. His musical ability and authenticity outshine any other worship leaders at the churches we've attended. Indeed, their Sunday services, specifically the worship music, surpass everything else, setting our expectations high as we visit other churches. Inevitably, every alternative falls short.

With the worship leader on lead guitar, he's supported by a talented team: backup guitar, bass guitar, drums, and keyboard, along with a couple of vocalists. They lead us for about forty minutes as we slide from one tune to another. Most are familiar to me; a few are new.

Some people dance with varying degrees of expression and ability, praising God with their movements. All who do, however, do so from their seats. No one moves to the aisle or goes to the front of the stage. I've seen both happen here in the past, but not today.

Unique in our experience of visiting churches is the kids' participation in worship. On one side of the stage stand a series of easels for kids to use to draw, creating art and expressing themselves as the congregation praises God. Other children wave kid-sized worship flags, often running back and forth in front of the stage in a physical display of worship. Occasionally, adults joined them in the past, but not today. Might they be too self-conscious? But the children are not. These kids don't limit their expressions of joy because of what others may think but have an unrestrained zeal to move with delight. Other children sit with their families, waving their flags under the watchful eye of their parents. This is a time of exultation.

CELEBRATING EASTER

As the music ends, the senior pastor stands for the first time. People know to expect the unexpected. "Today," he says in mock seriousness, "I want to address the systematic theology of Easter." Snickers abound as he continues his somber ruse.

At the expense of his professors, he pokes fun at his seminary training. His stories of his time on campus amuse the crowd. Today will be a celebration. Somber seriousness will have no place.

His tenor eases as he evokes C. S. Lewis and his classic *The Chronicles of Narnia*. They play a clip from the movie, showing Aslan's capture and being prepared for sacrifice. They stop the clip just before the scene becomes PG-13. This is "the ransom theory of atonement," he deadpans, holding his gaze until the crowd knows he's again mocking his formal theological training. Even though he didn't deserve it, "Aslan dies for Edmund".

"You are an idiot," he later yells. "And Jesus loves idiots," he adds with a smile. "Only God can take a crucifixion and turn it into a resurrection." Throughout his message he weaves in Scripture, often citing the book but not giving the chapter and verse, so I'm unable to note a single passage.

"Because of Jesus," he concludes, "we can make an impact wherever we are."

"Happy Easter!"

The service ends. The message lasted twenty-three minutes, with the whole service just over an hour. As the worship team plays, most people exit, though many stay to talk.

CELEBRATING COMMUNITY

We move slowly, allowing time for past friends to come up to talk. Many do. It's a delightful time of reunion: reconnecting, giving updates, and sharing life. We praise God for his work in this church family. We celebrated our Lord during the service. Now we celebrate community afterward. We tarry in conversation. When people arrive for the second service, we finally head out.

The service was good but quite restrained compared to their past Easter celebrations. There were no bouncing beach balls, no dancing in the aisles, and no spontaneous baptisms. It was more like other churches and less like their maverick past. This church is maturing and growing up; I'm sad.

Though we subconsciously use this church as our standard to evaluate all others, I realize that even it no longer matches our expectations. They too fall short. While our memories could be in error, it's more likely that they've changed. They've moved closer to the status quo and further away from their countercultural approach to worshiping God and doing church. The thrill is gone.

Such is often the case when young churches grow up.

Takeaway: To stand out for Jesus, maintain what makes your church unique and don't feel a need to conform to meet status quo expectations.

Questions:

- Are your church services a celebration? Should they be?
- How has your church changed in the past few years?
- Are these changes positive?
- What should your reaction be?

SHOULD CHURCHES LAST FOREVER?
GRAPPLING WITH LONGEVITY

When we visited Church #15 (An Outlier Congregation), they were at a crossroads. They finally bought a building for a permanent place of worship, renovated it, and moved in. They had also received their denomination's official permission to organize. Both were arduous tasks, and the people were tired. Some longed to rest, and others desired to push forward. The pastors realized this, and that day's service addressed it.

I also sensed that the ministers—a husband and wife duo—were tired too. They may likewise have been at a crossroads. Should they push forward, or is the better course to take a needed respite to recharge and prepare for what's next?

I wasn't concerned; I was sure they'd figure it out. Yet

when I wonder about them a few years later and try to visit their website for an update, it no longer exists. Their Facebook page has also been closed. When I try an online search, AI tells me it looks like they've been closed for about a year. That's all I can find.

I'm sad. They had so much to offer and seemed to do so many things well, but apparently it wasn't sustainable. It didn't last.

Longevity is a dilemma for churches. Just as with all organizations, churches have a life cycle—or at least they should.

Churches are organic, alive and growing. Hence the term *church planting*. When ministers go out to start a new church, it's often called a church plant. Just as with planting a seed in the ground to produce a crop, these ministers plant a church in the community. With God's grace, the planted church sprouts, grows, and matures. It produces a harvest. Yet, as with all living things, the church grows up, ages, and then slows down. Eventually it dies.

The only way for a church to continue indefinitely is for it to become an institution. Then it's no longer organic. It ceases to be alive. Though it often tries to function as if it were—with varying degrees of success—it's usually more akin to going through the motions.

As an institution, the church places an emphasis on their ongoing viability. Self-preservation becomes key. The result is that it looks inward and forgets to reach outward. It addresses the needs of members and forgets the needs of their surrounding community. Outreach becomes ineffective —or nonexistent.

Most people expect churches to live forever. They mourn when congregations close their doors.

Yet this may be the wrong perspective. Instead of praising longevity, we're better to celebrate a church that lived well—for making a tremendous kingdom impact during their existence, be it long or short.

Church #1 (A Friendly Place with a Homey Feel) was a small congregation with a doubtful future. They didn't make it. I'm not surprised by this, but I celebrate the effective way they had encouraged their small flock to pursue spiritual community.

Similarly, Church #11 (Charismatic Lite) has also apparently closed. Their website no longer exists, their former meeting place is empty, and they don't come up in any online searches. I applaud how they attracted people from larger churches who sought a more intimate community and a place to grow in their faith. They provided a space for them to belong.

Church #27 (A Charismatic Experience) also provided a space for spiritual community. Those gathered worshiped God passionately, prayed fervently, and loved one another without reservation. Though they have disappeared, a Spanish-speaking congregation now meets in their former space. Interestingly, this is the fourth church to meet there. We had visited the first three, two of which have since moved to other locations.

When we visited Church #34 (Acts Chapter Two), we heard an information-packed message about the Holy Spirit, starting with Pentecost and connecting to the Azusa Street Revival of 1906, which formed this church's DNA.

The sparsely attended service, however, totaled eleven. This included five from the visiting speaker's family. Subtracting them, along with Candy and me, left four regulars. One of them said, "We're in a rebuilding phase." In truth, they were on life support; they didn't make it.

Last on this list is Church #35 (A Well-Kept Secret). We stumbled upon them by accident. Our time there was both uncomfortable and intriguing. With several practices and traditions unfamiliar to us, we approached God from a fresh perspective. We worshiped God and proclaimed Jesus. After the service we enjoyed a time of exuberant community. Though their building still exists, the church that met there no longer does—at least not from what I can determine. But perhaps they live on at another location, and it's just another well-kept secret.

There may be other churches that closed as well, but it's challenging to know for sure. Some churches moved, and others changed their names. A surprising number did neither, but changed their web address, making it challenging to find them and learn their latest news.

Takeaway: Churches come and churches go, but how long

they last doesn't matter nearly as much as the impact they make while they're here.

Questions:

- What is your reaction when you hear about a church closing?
- What do you think about local churches having a life cycle?
- Have you ever attended a church that closed? How did you deal with it?
- Have you ever been part of a church plant? What was your experience?

CELEBRATE PERSISTENCE
SOME CHURCHES SURVIVE

Most of the churches we visited continue to meet, ministering to their congregations and reaching into their communities as they worship and serve God. This is a cause for celebration.

A handful of these churches we visited had bleak futures —at least from a human perspective. Despite their dire outlook, however, through God's grace and provisions they persevered and survived. They pressed on, and they continue in ministry.

Praise God!

Church #6 (A Quintessential Country Church), with their small attendance, aging demographics, and tiny offerings, seemed even more at risk than Church #1 (A Friendly Place with a Homey Feel). Yet Church #6 continues to minister to their small, rural community. They are an example of being faithful, even in the face of discouraging situations.

An even smaller gathering was Church #28 (Intriguing and Liturgical). Fascinated by their rituals, we visited a second time, which was better attended. Some of their practices perplexed me, yet their after-church community was precious. I'm delighted to know that their impact continues.

We visited Church #32 (Commitment Sunday and Celebration) right when they emerged from the darkest chapter in their history. It would have been easy for them to give up, shut their doors, and disperse. They did not. They persevered. We visited at the culmination of their rebirth. I'm so glad they're still around, worshiping God and serving their community.

A fourth congregation that survived despite my concerns was Church #33 (A Shepherd Cares for His Flock). Their minister faithfully served his small congregation, helping feed them both spiritually and physically. His commitment is admirable and worthy of emulation. I rejoice that the church is still there, along with their loyal leader.

We celebrate these churches—and all congregations that push forward when the prudent advice might be to give up. Their perseverance is admirable, and their kingdom impact —though not as wide as larger churches—is both deep and significant.

Takeaway: God commends those who are faithful in small things (Luke 16:10).

Questions:

- Do we celebrate churches for their size and numeric growth or their kingdom impact and spiritual growth? Might God's perspective be different?
- When have we tried to force a church, project, or initiative forward when God may have had other plans?
- Have we ever given up on something when God might have wanted us to press forward?

LEADERSHIP TRANSITIONS
CHANGE IS INEVITABLE
BUT THE OUTCOME ISN'T

Our visit to Church #12 (More Methodists, More Food) left us with many positive memories. An intriguing aspect of their gathering was that they had different worship formats throughout the month, varying in instrumentation and song selection. To fully experience them, we would need to return for a month-long visit.

I want to go back but am also concerned that showing up four weeks in a row would imply an intent to join their congregation. That would not be the case—unless God were to direct us otherwise. Instead, our goal would be to experience their full array of service formats, learning about the varied ways they worship God.

In researching this church, I discover that the minister has been there for six and a half years. I understand that the typical tenure for this denomination is seven. That means it's likely she will soon move on.

I consider what draws me to them.

The congregation is friendly, open, and inviting. I appreciate how the laity handles many aspects of the service. And their monthly potluck offers a time for fellowship and deeper connection, which seems to best happen in the presence of food. I expect these admirable traits will all continue.

Yet, what most attracts me is how the minister conducts the service. Reverent and sincere, she isn't flying through a set of rituals, as can too easily happen. Her demeanor draws me to God and helps me better engage in worship. In my experience, she does this better than any other.

When I check several months later, she's no longer there, and they're between pastors. Not having a regular minister in place doesn't concern me. All churches will go through this at some point, though I must admit my interest in returning diminishes. For all I know, their practice of varying their worship formats left with their minister.

A few weeks later, I talk with a young woman. She says she and her husband are helping a struggling church that is between ministers; they will handle the worship music. As she shares details, I realize she's talking about this church.

Leadership transitions are often difficult for churches, especially for solo pastorates. Often attendance drops and interest languishes. Other times, the congregation pulls together, striving to maintain what they had.

When the new minister arrives, some people inevitably leave, but new people usually show up. Sometimes those who left when the former pastor did will return.

Contrasted to this is Church #23 (They'll Be Fine). When we visited, we had missed their departing minister by a month. He had moved on, and they were in transition. That Sunday we witnessed the approval of their pastoral selection committee.

The people we talked to after the service were optimistic about their future. Though they missed their minister, they said he had prepared them well for this transition. Everything I witnessed that Sunday confirmed this. Aside from the actual message, the members handled everything else themselves. Not only did they cover all other aspects of the service, but they also functioned most admirably beforehand and especially in the fellowship time afterward.

I was sure they'd be fine, and they were.

Takeaway: Wise leaders prepare their congregations to function without them. Foolish leaders control every aspect, which trains their congregations to depend on them.

Questions:

- How prepared is your church to navigate a
  change in leadership?

- What would your reaction be if your pastor left?
- How well does your congregation function without your minister present?
- What can you do now to be better prepared for when a leadership transition occurs?

MOVING TOWARD A NEW NORMAL
AN OUTDOOR SERVICE

For our final consideration, we'll move beyond the original fifty-two churches to revisit one more to complete our discussion.

It's July 2020, and it's been four months since I've been to church on Sunday morning. It's not that I've lost my faith, have backslidden, or am pursuing a rebellious protest. Instead, it's because of Covid restrictions. With government mandates to avoid large gatherings, most churches responded by moving their services online and closing their doors to people. After four months of isolation, some churches reemerge as a place to gather.

Sadly, I've not missed it.

THREE REASONS TO GO TO CHURCH

A former minister once remarked that some people go to church for the music and put up with the sermon. Other people go for the sermon and put up with the music. At various times in my life, I've done both. Now I do neither. In recent years, I've shown up at church for the chance of experiencing community before and after the service.

Though I've listened to our church's online services most every Sunday, I've often wondered why. Remote worship and recorded sermons mean little to me. And from the distanced safety of my living room, interaction with others —aside from family—doesn't occur.

I want to say that I miss my friends at church ("The Postcard Church" from *Shopping for Church*). In truth, it's more accurate to say I miss my acquaintances. If you define a friend as someone you intentionally spend time with, then I have no friends at church. Church services are our only connection, and without a church gathering, we lose that singular point of contact. Therefore, it's an overreach to call these familiar faces at church my friends.

Emotionally, I miss their smiles, waves, and conversations. But now that I've gone without these things for a third of a year, their absence has left little of a void in my life.

CONNECTIONS AT LAST

Today we have our first opportunity to attend church for a Sunday morning gathering, but we're not going to our home church. They're proceeding with caution and aren't ready yet. Instead, we're going to another nearby church, one within walking distance ("The Closest Church" from *Shopping for Church*). They've been holding outdoor services for the past month. Some of our neighbors attend there, as well as one of Candy's coworkers. We expect to see familiar faces.

We could walk, but the predicted temperatures will hit the mid-90s today, with an accompanying high humidity. It's already in the low 80s, without a cloud in the sky. The fifteen-minute walk would surely leave us a sweaty mess and not feeling our best.

Our daughter and her family plan to meet us there. They arrive a bit before we do and have already claimed a spot in the shade on the right side of the stage. We join them, setting up our folding chairs. It's 9:30 in the morning, and the shade offers a welcome relief from the heat that has already formed.

The church website and Facebook page make no mention of social distancing or wearing masks, unlike most businesses and many other churches, which state strict guidelines for proper coronavirus etiquette. I'm quite willing to do the first but not the second since we're outside, especially given that my lone mask is in our other car.

It doesn't matter. No one—not even their church leaders —wears a mask. Yet everyone makes some effort at social distancing, avoiding hugs and handshakes, while conducting conversations at six or so feet apart. We have brief interactions with a few people, mostly those we know. Otherwise, we stay segregated in our family group, as do most other households.

OUTDOOR CHURCH

A portable stage sits on the east side of their building. A tent awning provides shade for those on the platform, while the rest of us sit in the open sun or rely on the shade of a few nearby trees. The sun, not yet near its peak, shines over the left shoulders of the people gathered. A gentle breeze provides a bit of pleasant relief.

One of our neighbors tells us that, given today's forecast, they'll have an abbreviated service. She serves as their worship leader. They're in between ministers, with their former one departing nine months ago and their new one arriving next week. Today we'll hear a guest speaker.

The worship leader stands behind a portable electric organ. She welcomes us and begins the first song. She's aided by two backup vocalists, a drummer, and a guitarist. As we sing, the words appear on monitors, which flank each side of the stage. We sing a couple of familiar choruses to a light pop sound.

One of their leaders gives announcements. He confirms

that, given today's forecast, "Our service will be shorter than usual." He adds that though we'll endure the heat and humidity for a while, we'll retreat to our air-conditioned cars and return to our air-conditioned homes. He's right.

And with that, he introduces us to the guest speaker.

THE STORY THAT GROUNDS YOU

Fifteen minutes into the service, the message begins. The sermon title appears on the monitors: "The Story That Grounds You, Exodus 13." The minister reads Exodus 13:1–16, encouraging us to follow along in our Bibles. Words do not appear on the monitors. I wonder why.

It's the Fourth of July weekend, and he links our country's celebration of independence to ancient Israel's Independence Day, as implied in the Exodus text. It's an interesting observation, but his inferences about Israel seem weak. He reviews the facts surrounding the departure of God's people from captivity in Egypt, but he offers no application. Or it could be that I miss it. I make only a few sermon notes, though I may be out of practice. It's been four months since I last did this.

The title, I guess, is the point: What is the story that grounds us?

The message takes twenty-five minutes, and we conclude the service with a final song. After the benediction, most people are quick to fold up their chairs and leave. A few tarry to talk, but these conversations don't last long. By the time we walk to our car, most people have already left, and the set-up crew has dismantled and stored the technology and tools used in today's service.

We arrive home at 10:30, one hour after the service began.

Takeaway: When your church must pivot—regardless of the reasons—be open and flexible.

Questions:

- Do you go to church for the music or the sermon? Or the community? Or another motivation?
- How can you help people whose reasons differ from yours?
- Do you take sermon notes? Why or why not? Should you?

WRAP UP
FINAL THOUGHTS ON
REVISITING 52 CHURCHES

To complete our revisit of churches, here are some concluding thoughts to wrap up our discussion:

SEEKING THE FULL PENTECOSTAL EXPERIENCE

You may wonder if I ever return a third time to Church #14 (The Pentecostal Perspective) for the full Pentecostal experience. I do not. Though they openly welcomed and embraced me on both visits, their theology rejects my understanding and practice of faith. At best, they deem me to be spiritually lacking. At worst, they see me as a heathen to convert.

With much I can learn from them about the Holy Spirit,

their judgment of me as a spiritual outsider pushes me away. Since I don't speak in tongues, they will never fully accept me.

I don't return.

A LACK OF SPIRITUAL GUMPTION

Though I plan to—and want to—go back to Church #21 (A New Kind of Church) for the full experience of their community on the first Saturday of the month, I never do. Initially, it's because of schedule conflicts. Later, we move away, making a return trip impractical.

Even so, there was one date when I could have gone but didn't. I lacked the spiritual gumption to push through and talked myself out of going. Still, I think about them, their ministry, and their gathering. I wonder about their impact on the surrounding community and the entire world.

LITURGY, GREETING WITH A HOLY KISS, AND THE HOLY SPIRIT

Of all the churches we visited, Church #28 (Intriguing and Liturgical) differs the most from our normal practices—or anything we've ever encountered. Their services are mysterious to me yet also strangely compelling. Enigma best describes it.

Part of me wants to return for a third visit, while another part of me can't figure out why. It may be that while my spirit is drawn to the mystical, my education steeps me in the logical. It's a dichotomy that both delights and perplexes me.

Though I think of them occasionally and wonder about a return trip, I never go.

CHANGED SCHEDULES

Recall the Sunday morning where we tried and failed twice to go to church (Church #27, A Charismatic Experience and Church #8, A Missed Opportunity). In both instances, we arrived at the stated, publicized times, only to encounter changed schedules.

This frustrates me, likely amplified because our home church did this multiple times during their first years of existence (Church #53, Home for Holy Week). They usually announced a shift in the schedule the Sunday before but failed to update their website or phone greeting. People who weren't there the previous week had no way of knowing the time had changed. They'd arrive according to the past schedule and be understandably mad.

Once the lone notice came from a midweek email message, which only those on the email list received, accounting for a fraction of the typical attendance.

In all these cases—both at these two churches and at our home church—those on the inside knew of the change in plans, while those on the outside didn't.

MINISTERS RETIRE

The minister at Church #4 (Successfully Melding Contemporary and Traditional) is someone I've known most of my life, the older brother of my best friend in junior high.

One Sunday my mother visits this church and learns the minister will soon retire. The news shocks me—though it shouldn't.

I have no plans to retire; I hope and pray that I'll be able to write for the rest of my life—until the day I die. When you love the work you do, there's no reason to stop. Besides, God has called me to write for him, and I have many more books to complete.

Given my personal perspective, when I hear of someone near my age retiring, I'm often taken aback. Yet most people —including ministers—will one day retire.

This minister is my primary draw to the church. The same goes for my mother. Knowing he's no longer there gives us little reason to return.

CHURCH BUILDINGS

When we first visited Church #2 (Growing Deeper, Not Wider), they met in a space at a small strip mall. When we revisited them, they met in a public school building. They had bought property and were planning to build a facility there.

They did indeed build and move into a new facility, but it wasn't on the property they had purchased. It was at a different location, about a half mile west of Churches #4 and #5 (Catholics are Christians Too).

Church #38 (A Refreshing Time) also met in a public school building. They too have moved from that to their own building.

The third one of the fifty-two churches that met in a school building was Church #25 (Embarking on a Metamorphosis). Technically, they closed, but functionally they merged with another church.

According to plan, both churches suspended their Sunday gatherings for a time as they prepared to combine forces and move forward together. Though the transition took much longer than anyone expected, the pastor of Church #25 led the new group, which met in the former building of the other church. To distinguish themselves from either of the former congregations, they rallied under a new name.

The result was a new, growing church with their own building.

Church #43 (A Welcoming Church with Much to Offer) also met in a rented space. They likewise built a facility. It was on land they had purchased many years ago, at last seeing the fruition of their long-ago vision. Interestingly, prior to the construction, they sometimes held special outdoor meetings on this property, such as on the week after our third visit to their church.

FINAL THOUGHT

In *Revisiting 52 Churches* we didn't cover each one; that would have been tedious. But we considered half of them—either directly or incidentally. In doing so, we focused on those that offered additional insights or meaningful lessons to ponder. We physically revisited most of these churches, while we mentally revisited the rest.

In doing so, we celebrated their successes and grew through their shortcomings.

Takeaway: Just as churches change, so do we. It's best when we can do so together.

Questions:

- Which of these churches do you most connect with?
- What can you learn from them?
- What can you celebrate?
- How can you thank God and worship him as a result?

If you liked *Revisiting 52 Churches,* please leave a review online. Your review will help others discover this book and encourage them to read it too.

Thank you.

52 CHURCHES SUMMARY

Here is a listing of all fifty-two churches and a brief overview of the congregations covered in the book *52 Churches*.

Church #1, A Friendly Place with a Homey Feel: This church has no online presence, as well as an uninviting exterior. But the people inside are friendly, and we feel at home—mostly.

Church #2, Growing Deeper, Not Wider: The church is three years old and meets in a strip mall. Their goal is to "grow deeper, not wider." Everything about this church is the opposite of last week.

Church #3, It Only Hurts When You Care: The third church is more established like Church #1 but more midsized like Church #2. We visit them on a difficult weekend for their congregation.

Church #4, Successfully Melding Contemporary and Traditional: This church's Facebook page—they have no website—says their "services are informal with a blend of hymns and contemporary music."

Church #5, Catholics Are Christians Too: When I tell people we're visiting area churches, I specify *Christian*, but they often hear *Protestant*. It surprises them to learn we'll visit Catholic gatherings too. Today is our first.

Church #6, A Quintessential Country Church: This small church didn't come up in our online research, but we have driven past it. All we know is their name and service time.

Church #7, The New Church: I suspect this church is only a couple years old. I later learn they're an outgrowth of a small group.

Church #8, A Grand Experiment: This week we visit our third new church. It's a grand experiment, one quite radical from their conservative denominational roots.

Church #9, Methodists Know How to Cook: Today, we'll go to a United Methodist church, our first visit to a widely recognized denomination.

Church #10, A Special Father's Day Message: Today's church has no website, and their Facebook page only links to their denomination's website.

Church #11, Charismatic Lite: The trendy website of this church gives no indication of their focus or affiliation. In contrast, their Facebook page says they're charismatic.

Church #12, More Methodists, More Food: Next up is another United Methodist Church. It's a rural congregation and not on the way to anywhere we go, so we didn't know it existed until we stumbled on it.

Church #13, A Dedicated Pastor Team: This church has no website and a blank Facebook page. The lack of information online discourages me.

Church #14, The Pentecostal Perspective: The church website doesn't give their affiliation, but the pastor's bio implies they're Pentecostal. Their Facebook page, however, prominently confirms this.

Church #15, An Outlier Congregation: Their website says we'll find "a laid-back, coffeehouse atmosphere" with "an unconventional setting where a blend of people, of all ages, from all walks of life, can gather and feel at home." This is my kind of church. It's an outlier congregation in a mainline denomination.

Church #16, Something's Missing: This nondenominational church meets in a public school auditorium. They offer much, but their execution is a bit lacking.

Church #17, A Doubleheader: This church has a contemporary service followed by a traditional one. We'll go to both.

Church #18, Revisiting Roman Catholicism: Today we visit our second Roman Catholic Church. I'm excited—and nervous.

Church #19, A Near Miss: With no website and a phone line that doesn't work, we assume this church, listed only in a computer-compiled online directory, either no longer exists or never did. The sign in front of their building is the only reason we know the service time.

Church #20, Different Language, Same God: This week is another doubleheader, but with a twist. First is a Mandarin worship service and English Sunday school, followed by an English worship service and Mandarin Sunday school.

Church #21, A New Kind of Church: Most of this church's ministry happens on Saturday. The Sunday service is for those they meet during their Wednesday evening street ministry.

Church #22, A Caring Community: This church meets in a newer, contemporary building. It's most inviting.

Church #23, They'll Be Fine: Last Sunday was their minister's last day. Other area clergy have great respect for him. I wish I could have met him.

Church #24, Good but Not Typical: This church resulted when three dying congregations merged a quarter century ago, but with a worship team of teens brought in, today isn't a normal service.

Church #25, Embarking on a Metamorphosis: The website of this church shows captivating photos of their worship team, implying high energy and an edgy sound.

Church #26, An Unknown Situation: A friend tells us about a new African American congregation. Once again, we'll be minorities at church.

Church #27, A Charismatic Experience: This charismatic church meets in an old, run-down building, originally built for shared-tenant use. It looks abandoned and forms our first impression.

Church #28, Intriguing and Liturgical: We learn of this church when we spot their name in a local paper's church directory. Still, we struggle to confirm their meeting time.

Church #29, Led by Laity: Their minister is gone this week, and the congregation handles all aspects of the service.

Church #30, Misdirected and Frustrated: After fifty agonizing minutes they say, "Thanks for coming. The service will start in about ten minutes." That's when we realized they tricked us into attending Sunday school—and it wasn't a good one.

Church #31, A Day of Contrasts: This church offers a mix of old with new, contemporary with traditional, and public friendliness with personal indifference.

Church #32, Commitment Sunday and Celebration: This church has been homeless for a while, but they moved into their own space last week. Today they celebrate God's faithfulness on a trying journey.

Church #33, A Shepherd Cares for His Flock: Even though this church is only nine miles from our house, the contrast between their lives and mine is stark. These people live in poverty.

Church #34, Acts Chapter Two: Today's destination is a charismatic church. We've not been to many so I'm excited for the experience.

Church #35, A Well-Kept Secret: This church didn't come up in our online search or in the local directory of churches. We stumbled on them while driving to another church.

Church #36, The Surprise: We walk inside to an empty lobby and head toward an amplified sound. We slink into a back row. We're confused by what's happening.

Church #37, Another Small Church: This church looks abandoned. With only two other cars, today promises to be another tiny gathering.

Church #38, A Refreshing Time: The church meets in a middle school's all-purpose room. Large portable signs direct us to the entrance.

Church #39, A Great Way to End the Year: With

Sunday falling between Christmas and New Year's Day, I have low expectations for today's service.

Church #40, No Time to Return: Our destination is a church we've heard of often but know little about. Our favorable impressions suggest a thriving, dynamic congregation. After the service they invite us back. I want to say yes, but our schedule won't permit it.

Church #41, People Make the Difference: The newer building doesn't look like a typical church. The sanctuary is open and inviting, with a comfortable feel.

Church #42, High Expectations and Great Disappointment: I've heard a great deal about the minister and this church. I've wanted to visit for a long time.

Church #43, A Welcoming Church with Much to Offer: Located in a building with shared tenant space, this church has an inviting location, easily accessible, with nearby parking.

Church #44, A Familiar Place: We attended this church years ago. This won't be a visit as much as a reunion.

Church #45, Another Doubleheader: Today we'll enjoy another doubleheader: a traditional service followed by a contemporary one.

Church #46, False Assumptions: The sprawling facility provides an impressive view from a distance. Their larger, new building suggests a thriving, dynamic community.

Church #47, Significant Interactions: When we arrive, one member provides needed information, leaving us informed about what to expect and prepared to worship.

Church #48, Small, Simple, and Satisfying: The church's pastor is out of town, and the laity leads the entire service.

Church #49, Large and Anonymous: This church is huge, the largest so far. Yet bigger isn't always better.

Church #50, Saturday Mass: A few months ago, we went to church on Saturday morning. Now we head off for a Saturday evening mass.

Church #51, The Megachurch: I'm both excited and apprehensive about visiting our area's largest church, but they give us a grand welcome, and we have a great experience.

Church #52, Playing it Safe: Our destination is not a church to visit but a revisit, returning to the congregation we were part of a decade ago.

Church #53, Home for Holy Week: It's Easter and we're returning home to our church, the people we love and miss. This marks our first Sunday here since last Easter. [Church #53 is the last one in *52 Churches* and the first one in *More Than 52 Churches*.]

FOR SMALL GROUPS, SUNDAY SCHOOL, AND CLASSES

Revisiting 52 Churches makes an ideal discussion guide for small groups, Sunday School, and classes. To prepare for the conversation, read the assigned chapters of this book before you meet.

When you get together, pray and ask for Holy Spirit insight.

Discuss the key points of the chapters, explore the take-away items, and answer the questions.

- Celebrate the areas your church does well.
- Consider a weakness that needs improvement.
- Determine what you can do to bring about positive change.

End by asking God to help you apply what you've learned.

May God bless you as you discuss this book and explore how to apply it to your faith practices.

ABOUT PETER DEHAAN

Peter DeHaan wants to change the world one word at a time. His books and blog posts discuss God, the Bible, and church, geared toward spiritual seekers and church dropouts. Many people feel church has let them down, and Peter seeks to encourage them as they search for a place to belong.

But he's not afraid to ask tough questions or make religious people squirm. He's not trying to be provocative. Instead, he seeks truth, even if it makes people uncomfortable. Peter urges Christians to push past the status quo and reexamine how they practice their faith in every part of their lives.

Peter earned his doctorate, awarded with high distinction, from Trinity College of the Bible and Theological Seminary. He lives with his wife in beautiful Southwest Michigan and wrangles crossword puzzles in his spare time.

A lifelong student of Scripture, Peter wrote the 1,000-page website ABibleADay.com to encourage people to explore the Bible, the greatest book ever written. His popular blog, at PeterDeHaan.com, addresses biblical Christianity to build a faith that matters.

Read his blog, receive his newsletter, and learn more at PeterDeHaan.com.

BOOKS BY PETER DEHAAN

VISITING CHURCHES SERIES

52 Churches

The 52 Churches Workbook

More Than 52 Churches

The More Than 52 Churches Workbook

Visiting Online Church

Shopping for Church

40-DAY BIBLE STUDY SERIES

Dear Theophilus (the Gospel of Luke)

Acts Bible Study

Isaiah Bible Study

Minor Prophets Bible Study

Job Bible Study

Living Water (John)

Love Is Patient (1 and 2 Corinthians)

Revelation Bible Study

1, 2, & 3 John Bible Study

Hebrews Bible Study

James and Jude Bible Study

Matthew Bible Study

1 & 2 Peter Bible Study

Mark Bible Study

Romans Bible Study

Paul's Short Epistles Bible Study

HOLIDAY CELEBRATION DEVOTIONALS

The Advent of Jesus

The Passion of Jesus (Lent)

The Victory of Jesus (Easter)

The Ministry of Jesus

Thanksgiving with Jesus

New Year with Jesus

BIBLE CHARACTER SKETCHES SERIES

Women of the Bible

The Friends and Foes of Jesus

Old Testament Sinners and Saints

More Old Testament Sinners and Saints

Heroes and Heavies of the Apocrypha

OTHER BOOKS

Elephant God

Jesus's Broken Church

Martin Luther's 95 Theses (formerly *95 Tweets*)

The Christian Church's LGBTQ Failure

Bridging the Sacred-Secular Divide (formerly *Woodpecker Wars*)

Beyond Psalm 150

For the latest list of all Peter's books, go to
PeterDeHaan.com/nonfiction.